ns through Chimayó

Querencias Series

Miguel A. Gandert
and Enrique R. Lamadrid,
Series Editors

Querencia is a popular term in the Spanish-speaking world used to express a deeply rooted love of place and people. This series promotes a transnational, humanistic, and creative vision of the U.S.-Mexico borderlands based on all aspects of expressive culture, both material and intangible.

Also available in the Querencias Series:

Enduring Acequias: Wisdom of the Land, Knowledge of the Water by Juan Estevan Arellano

Hotel Mariachi: Urban Space and Cultural Heritage in Los Angeles by Enrique R. Lamadrid and Catherine L. Kurland; Photographs by Miguel A. Gandert

Sagrado: A Photopoetics Across the Chicano Homeland by Spencer R. Herrera and Levi Romero; Photographs by Robert Kaiser

Chasing Dichos through Chimayó

Don J. Usner

UNIVERSITY OF NEW MEXICO PRESS · ALBUQUERQUE

© 2014 by Don J. Usner
All rights reserved. Published 2014
Printed in the United States of America
19 18 17 16 15   2 3 4 5 6

Library of Congress Cataloging-in-Publication Data

Usner, Donald J.
  Chasing dichos through Chimayó / Don J. Usner.
      pages cm. — (Querencias series)
  Includes bibliographical references and index.
  ISBN 978-0-8263-5523-2 (cloth : alk. paper) — ISBN 978-0-8263-5524-9 (electronic)
 1. Chimayo (N.M.)—Social life and customs. 2. Folklore—New Mexico—Chimayo.
3. Oral tradition—New Mexico—Chimayo. 4. Proverbs, Spanish—New Mexico—Chimayo.
5. Spanish poetry—New Mexico—Chimayo. 6. Chimayo (N.M.)—Biography.
7. Extended families—New Mexico—Chimayo. 8. Community life—New Mexico—Chimayo.
9. Chimayo (N.M.)—Description and travel. I. Title.
  F804.C48U86 2014
  398.209789'52—dc23
                          2014028863

DESIGNED BY Lila Sánchez
COMPOSED IN Adobe Garamond Pro 11.5/15.5; Display type is Brioche
COVER PHOTOS BY Don J. Usner

Contents

Prologue: Dichos, Performance, and Place
    ENRIQUE R. LAMADRID   vii

Introduction: Language at the Heart of Place   1

Esequiel and Magdalena in La Cuchilla   15
    DICHOS ABOUT MORTALITY   29

Tomasita's Chile Colorado from the Plaza de Abajo   31
    DICHOS ABOUT FRIENDSHIP AND ENMITY   38

Lorencito in the Plaza del Cerro   41
    DICHOS ABOUT FATE AND HARDSHIP   46

Benerito on La Otra Banda   51
    DICHOS ABOUT CHARACTER   56

Grabielita in Ranchitos   59
    DICHOS ABOUT CHARACTER   63

Esequiel in Los Ojuelos   67
    DICHOS ABOUT CHARACTER   71

Juan Trujillo and the Capilla de San Antonio del Potrero   75
    DICHOS ABOUT CHARACTER   83

Alonzo's Horses in Los Ojuelos   87
    DICHOS ABOUT CHARACTER   92

Santos Ortiz's House   95
    DICHOS ABOUT CHARACTER   100

Aaron Martínez in Los Ranchos   103
    DICHOS ABOUT CHARACTER   108

El Oratorio de San Buenaventura   111
    DICHOS ABOUT CHARACTER   118

A Pachanga in Rincón de los Trujillos	121
DICHOS ABOUT CHARACTER	127
Adiós Andariego	131
DICHOS ABOUT CHARACTER	135
Esequiel Takes a Spin	137
DICHOS ABOUT CHARACTER	142
Salomón	145
DICHOS ABOUT HEALTH	148
Don Patricio Cruz's House on the Hill	151
DICHOS ABOUT TRUTH	155
Narciso Trujillo in Los Pachecos	159
DICHOS ABOUT LOOKS AND APPEARANCE	165
The Capilla de Santa Rita in Chimayó Abajo	169
CONSEJOS (COUNSEL OR ADVICE)	177
Tom Montoya and the Maytag Roller	183
DICHOS ABOUT WORK AND MONEY	186
Wolfie and Another Corona	189
DICHOS ABOUT LOVE AND FAMILY	198
Grabielita on La Pascua	201
DICHOS ABOUT CHILDREN AND CHILD REARING	207
At the Campo Santo on Memorial Day	211
DICHOS ABOUT FAITH	217
Tomasita's Green Chile	221
DICHOS ABOUT FOOD	225
Postscript	229

Prologue

Dichos, Performance, and Place

The incorporation of proverbs into oral performance and literary expression is a tradition deeply rooted in Spanish language and culture. Generally known as *dichos* (sayings) and *refranes* (refrains), they are small poems whose metaphors and measured turns lend cultural and moral authority to the conversations of ordinary speakers and writers. From time immemorial they have served teachers, prophets, parents, and peers. Since medieval times, people have been compelled to gather them up in collections known as *refraneros*, hoping to harvest their wisdom.

Like a bouquet of wild flowers, they are picked from the meadow, their natural oral context, and set aside so all may admire their beauty. But of course they soon wilt. The challenge for poets, scholars, and storytellers has always been how to recontextualize these minimalist masterpieces. In the community of listeners and readers the greatest prestige belongs not to collectors, but to those with the talent of deploying proverbs with skill and wit. They are the *dichosos*, literally the "fortunate ones" who have mastered this age-old repertory of sayings and who can compose new ones for special occasions. Don Quijote's rustic pal Sancho Panza may be lazy, but he is a dichoso, a master of oral tradition. Amazingly enough, the dichos on his lips at every turn of the road are the very same ones we also use in our own equally complicated times.

"Language at the Heart of Place" is the poetic invocation that Don and Stella Chávez Usner use for their lifelong compilation of the globally dispersed, locally performed miniature poems known to Hispanos Nuevomexicanos as dichos or refranes. The collection of new and old sayings is interspersed with deep reflections on extended family and place through memoir and stunning photo portraits. Rather than salting away dusty lists of proverbs, Usner captures the cultural geography and oral genealogy of Chimayó in vibrant conversation with community elders.

For the Querencias Series
ENRIQUE R. LAMADRID

Benigna Ortega Chávez, Plaza del Cerro, 1995.

Introduction

Language at the Heart of Place

Con buenas palabras no hay mal entendedor.
With good words, there is no one who misunderstands.

Chimayó is one of the most mythologized, misunderstood—and, some would say, maligned—places in New Mexico. On one hand, it holds a place in the popular imagination as housing the "Lourdes of America," a reference (growing increasingly cliché) to the annual Good Friday pilgrimage to the Santuario de Chimayó, a nineteenth-century church where people trek by the thousands to receive the blessings of holy earth. Because of this legendary holy site, Chimayó is often exalted as a place of deep personal revelation, spiritual transformation, and outright miraculous healing. Visitors from far and near report feelings of deep peace, tranquility, joy—even bliss—when they visit the church and its environs. They pen testimonials and post photographs on the walls in the room where they scoop out the holy earth from the *posito*, a small pit in the earthen floor. They take the dirt to rub on their bodies, drink or eat, place on windowsills, or carry in plastic bags to intensive care units, senior centers, mental health facilities—wherever suffering calls for alleviation or despair seeks hope. They also leave behind photos of loved ones in need or recently deceased, asking for the divine intercession of the Santo Niño, a holy figure whose effigy is ensconsed in a shrine near near the posito.

New Mexicans and visitors from afar also celebrate Chimayó's weaving tradition, the potently flavorful chile grown there, and the local restaurant, where margaritas and pungent chile compete with the church's holy dirt as tourist draws. Some of New Mexico's finest artists reside here, finding inspiration in a centuries-long tradition of folk art and in the light and land. Chimayó's striking setting and cultural heritage have earned it a leading place along the tourist circuits of the Southwest. A prominent travel magazine declared in 2012 that Chimayó is one of the world's "sixteen most picturesque villages," an elite group of towns chosen for their "picture-perfect views and suspended-in-time charm."

Travel writers are wont to gush about Chimayó in terms like these, but at the same time, the media often sensationalize the plight of Chimayó as a haven for crime and violence. Lurid tales of every sort of criminal behavior conjure up a place quite different from a holy land. Instead, they paint a picture of profound social malaise and a dark downward spiral of family and community breakdown. Often repeated is the statistic that Río Arriba County, which comprises more than half of Chimayó, for decades has logged one of the highest overdose-related death rates in the United States, with most of those deaths attributed to heroin abuse. This has led some to label Chimayó the heroin capital of the Southwest. Some nod their heads and comment that this dark history goes back Spanish Colonial times, when Chimayó was a penal colony—a gross overstatement based on historic documents that mention that criminals were once banished to Chimayó and other places on the periphery of the colony.

Then there's the "poverty," a constant cause for hand-wringing and a source of more grim statistics. In New Mexico—one of the poorest states in the union, according to per capita income data—Río Arriba is among the poorest counties. Chimayó is often referred to as a third world country in the midst of the richest nation on earth.

Because of these striking contradictions, the ethos of Chimayó plays out as a juxtaposition of good and evil, a Janus-faced caricature of a place that is at once a touchstone for spiritual enlightenment and an epicenter of poverty and social dysfunction. People often ask how this can be, how such stark contrasts can exist side by side in the small valley. Many theories have been proposed to explain this contraposition, but perhaps my late friend Víctor Perera summed it up best when he compared Chimayó to his native Guatemala. "I think the darkest dark is always attracted to the brightest light," he said, and while that falls short of explanation, it makes a kind of philosophic sense.

In any case, this view of Chimayó only scratches the surface of a place that is much more complex. Three thousand people live beyond the two highways that confine the experience of most visitors. Among them reside all kinds of people—weavers and *santeros*, scientists and laborers, housewives, farmers, business people, and, yes, a fair share of unemployed people. Also among them live saints and sinners, just as in any community—and every individual must admit to harboring both virtuous and wicked tendencies. These Chimayosos inhabit the Santa Cruz Valley from the foothills of the Sangre de Cristo Mountains downstream to the rural community of La Puebla, concentrated around old neighborhood centers called *plazas*. Each plaza has its own stories and characters. A deep history—and a kind of richness that isn't reflected in economic data—resonates here, in the language, the buildings, the people, and the land itself.

This historical face of Chimayó has held me rapt for most of my life, led me to research and write a master's thesis and two books, inspired me to make Chimayó my home for fifteen years, and still compels me to visit Chimayó often. Every trip I take there is like a pilgrimage, but I go for more than the holy dirt. I stop at the santuario often enough, but many other aspects of Chimayó draw me back again and again to explore places and meet people in the heart of this complicated, rich area. It is near at hand to the metropolitan areas of Santa Fe and Albuquerque, and it lies well within the borders of the United States, but to go into the community and meet the people is to experience a place utterly apart from those cities—and even farther removed from the rest of the country in the twenty-first century.

My journeys to Chimayó began in childhood, when I went there with my family to visit my grandmother, Benigna Chávez, who lived only a stone's throw from the house where she was born in 1898. The trips to Chimayó in the 1952 Dodge stuffed with kids carried us far away from our day-to-day world in Los Alamos, where my father worked at the Los Alamos Scientific Laboratory (now the Los Alamos National Laboratory) and we lived and went to school. During the summer, my siblings and I took turns staying for days or weeks at a time with Grandma, who was widowed and lived alone. We were sent to keep her company and help her with daily tasks, but we had ample opportunity to wander in the hills, ramble on rough dirt roads through farm fields, and jump in the hay in ancient, teetering barns. For some of my siblings, the time in Chimayó was a kind of banishment, but for me, it was a magical escape from Los Alamos.

The differences between these two places where I grew up—Los Alamos and Chimayó—were manifold. Chimayó is a place with history, but Los Alamos is a place without much, and this was especially true in 1957, when I was born. Established hurriedly in the midst of some of the most rooted communities in the United States, Los Alamos arrived as an alien colony, its residents transplanted there from all corners of the globe for one narrow purpose: to design and build an atomic bomb. It was a military occupation, as the army and scientists established the Los Alamos Scientific Laboratory practically overnight. In contrast, Chimayó grew slowly in situ by the toil of many generations of Hispanos whose purpose in being there was to raise their crops and livestock and take care of their families.

These differences played out in myriad ways for me. In Chimayó I kept busy with chores that were quite different from my Los Alamos duties. Grandma assigned me not to take out the trash, but to burn it in a barrel behind her house. I didn't mow a lawn or water one with garden hoses. Instead, I swept the dirt *patio* beside the house and lent old men a hand in directing water through small *acequias* (irrigation ditches) to rows of chile and corn. Grandma might ask for help picking fruit from ancient trees or slicing and spreading the plucked prizes on screens under the *portal* to dry, but we didn't go to a grocery store to pick cans off a shelf. (In any case, going to town to shop was not an option, since Grandma never learned to drive and didn't own a car—except for her father's defunct 1932 Chevy, which sat in a garage and only moved when my brother and I spirited it away on misadventures.)

This place of summer getaway looked different, too. The roads in Chimayó weren't paved or straight, and none of the houses were quite square. There were no stoplights or street names. The people built and maintained their own adobe houses or inherited them from a long line of *antepasados*, who also built them by hand. Many of the mud-coated buildings didn't even have foundations. Although Grandma and most of her neighbors had gas heaters that ran on propane delivered by truck, winter heat in most homes came from woodstoves and fireplaces that filled the air with the fragrance of piñón and juniper smoke. Firewood was stacked outside each house, each stick carefully used for maximum efficiency. Cranky, shallow wells and a single community water system (reaching only a few dozen homes) delivered drinking water some of the time, but not always, and what came out of pipes in private wells was often discolored and tasted odd. A lot of people still drew drinking water from the acequias, and outhouses were the norm.

Los Alamos, on the other hand, was designed and built as a modern, planned town, with a landscaped community center and well-designed infrastructure. Houses were built by contractors, not by their owners, and were placed on concrete footings anchored several feet into solid volcanic tuff. They neatly lined the paved streets, which had smooth sidewalks and curbs, and each road bore a prosaic name or number (we lived on Alabama Avenue and then 36th Street). In my early years, the residents didn't own these cookie-cutter houses; they belonged to the Atomic Energy Commission, and the occupants paid no rent to stay in them. It was essentially free housing—a far cry from the homeowner-built-and-owned casitas in the Valley below Los Alamos. Men in gray trucks from the Zia Company came to fix anything that broke. They painted the walls every few years. They even mowed the lawns.

In contrast to smoky corner fireplaces or battered woodstoves, Los Alamos homes had central heating fueled by natural gas that came through a pipeline stretching from the faraway San Juan Basin. Controlled by the most modern thermostats, these heaters chugged in our homes all winter long, and we paid no attention to the heat wastefully pouring out of the single-pane windows. A powerful system drew water from deep wells and moved it with massive electric pumps uphill to town. This expensive system watered tidy lawns that were carefully delineated by bright chain link fences.

Cultural differences between the places were also dramatic. In Chimayó we found ourselves among relatives who knelt in humility at the shrine of holy dirt in the adobe recesses of the santuario and tilled the land to plant tongue-biting chile peppers. With our neighbors and relatives named Ortega, Trujillo, Jaramillo, Naranjo, Baca, and Martínez, we reveled in the sound of gurgling acequias, the scent of rain-soaked earth, the flavors of chile, beans, and *papas fritas*. We walked the dirt roads knowing that our *tías* and *tíos* and *primos* lived on every side. Everyone shared a common history of struggle and survival in a difficult land. There we knew intimately a whole slew of *viejitos* (elders), all of them honored, loved, and included in family events and affairs. Indeed, the viejitos presided as revered matriarchs and patriarchs. Some endeavored to teach us the names of ancestors long gone, so that we could recite at least parts of genealogies stretching back to the family origins in various regions of Spain.

In the Lourdes of America, celebrations included performances by masked Matachines dancers and processions of Penitentes reenacting the Passion of Christ. Banners in parades bore images of the Virgin or other holy figures. ("Penitentes" is the common, if inappropriate name for the confraternity more properly known as Los Hermanos de Nuestro Padre Jesús Nazareno, a men's religious society common to many communities in New Mexico). Families were anything but nuclear, spreading out to embrace multiple threads of relation through blood, marriage, and *compadrazgo*, another kind of nonfamilial thread that bound together extended networks. People in Chimayó were rooted deeply in place, connected to the land and to each other in complex and tightly interwoven patterns.

In Los Alamos, the company town, the sound of explosives detonating and the blare of a loud signal horn marked the passage of time. Boosters proudly advertised Los Alamos as the "Atomic City." The image of a mushroom cloud was emblazoned on license plates and painted on banners in holiday parades. The local fast-pitch baseball team was called the Atomic Bombers. Daily life revolved around a heady weapons-development mission, and we played with unrelated kids whose parents came from afar to labor behind fences on projects that they couldn't speak about. We mingled with kids named Dudziak, Rutherford, Nafziger, Calvin, Brophy, and Sherwood—most of them from small families organized on the nuclear-family model (with "nuclear" having a peculiar resonance). Most people had no connection to the land or each other. Family names told nothing of relationships. Old people were almost completely absent. Grandparents lived in distant cities and had little influence on their grandchildren's lives. Many of my friends in Los Alamos couldn't name an ancestor beyond a generation or two, and some knew grandparents only through telephone calls.

Further complicating these contrasts and contradictions was my mixed ethnic heritage. My mom had married a *gabacho* (foreigner), as the Chimayosos called my father (with no disrespect), shortly after World War II. Over the next fifteen years, out of Mom and Dad's union came a covey of children who, superficially at least, bore genetics of Hispanic and "Anglo" derivation. The truth of our ethnic identity is much more convoluted than that, though. Tangled into a long Hispanic pedigree going back thirteen generations in New Mexico, my mother carries strains of Irish as well as a trace (*una gotita*—just a little drop, as my grandmother used to say) of Native American parentage. (The story goes that her great-grandfather some eight times over, Pedro Durán y Chávez II, married a half-Zuni Indian.) My father also completely lacked real "Anglo" ancestry. He came from complex French-German-Irish-Hispanic (Cuban) roots in the melting pot of New Orleans.

Notwithstanding these subtleties, some viejitos from Chimayó affectionately referred to me and my siblings as *coyotes*, a term they used for the offspring of any New Mexico Hispanic and a gabacho—although, like the coyote character of myth, the meaning of this and other class and ethnic categories in northern New Mexico is always shifting. In Spanish Colonial times, "coyote" referred to the progeny of an Indian and a Spaniard or, alternatively, to a child of any European-born father and a New Mexican Indian. Nowadays, "coyote" has sinister overtones, especially for immigrants crossing illegally into the United States from Mexico, who often must hire smugglers called coyotes, many of them of questionable character, to get them across the border. But in northern New Mexico, many people still regard "coyote" as a not-unkind reference to a person of mixed heritage.

On one side of my family lineage we may be called coyotes, Anglos, gabachos, gringos, or whites, while on the other it's Hispanic, Latino, Mexican, Spanish American, or Chicano—and much worse terms have been thrown at us from both sides. All these epithets remain controversial, and although I don't mind being called a coyote, the label rankles others, including my mother. She says emphatically that we're all Americans and that's that.

In any case, experiencing two worlds while growing up enriched my life experience, but for some reason I felt compelled to push back strongly against the status quo on "the Hill" of Los Alamos. One of the ways to do this was to retreat into a Chimayó identity. This was easy to do. For all its anachronisms, Chimayó seemed to offer a more balanced way of being, and I wasn't alone in seeing in it and other land-oriented communities of northern New Mexico an alternative to the mainstream culture norms of the day. Droves of counterculturalists flocked here to found communes in the rural landscape amid the old Hispanic communities, seeking an antidote for the malaise they felt in urban America in the 1960s and '70s. For New Mexicans, it was amusing to watch as the "hippies" came from all corners of the country, dressed up in a kind of Old World peasant garb and seeking to recreate a rural, communal lifestyle—right alongside communities that had been living just such an existence for centuries. For my siblings and me to connect with our Old World village and find relief from the hubbub and confusion of Cold War America (as expressed in the isolated anomaly of Los Alamos), all we had to do was to drive down from the Hill to Grandma's house in the Valley.

It was a delight to escape to Chimayó, but at the same time reconciling the stark differences between my two hometowns proved to be something of a conundrum for me. Although there were a few other coyotes trapped in Los Alamos, I felt isolated from peers. It was a challenge to find acceptance in either place that I called home. Some neighbors in the Valley envied my siblings and me because we enjoyed the advantages of the financially secure families who lived in Los Alamos and worked at the laboratory; you might say they felt we were born with plutonium spoons in our mouths. At the same time, peers in Los Alamos sometimes openly derided the Valley culture as backward and inferior. Since I lacked a Hispanic surname, my Los Alamos friends often didn't know of my connection to Chimayó, and they were embarrassingly candid with racial jokes and innuendos that mocked Hispanics from the Valley; at the same time, my non-Hispanic surname prompted suspicion among my Chimayó peers.

My siblings and I learned the coyote shuffle, a clever dance back and forth across the tracks, slipping from one guise to another and back. Doing the dance required, among other skills, negotiating the language differences between Los Alamos and Chimayó. In the Valley everyone spoke a richly colloquialized, New Mexican variant of Spanish. Grandma and my mother switched from English and Spanish and back seamlessly, but many of the Chimayó viejitos spoke only Spanish. Overhearing their conversations amplified the sense of being in a place and time vastly different from Los Alamos—or just about anywhere else. It intrigued me that people in my own extended family communicated in a language the schools taught as "foreign." Teachers in those schools didn't teach the dialect I heard in my family, and my parents forbade us to repeat the Spanish we heard because they believed that doing so would diminish our facility with English or would inculcate us with a coarse local dialect of Spanish.

One year in high school I enrolled in an introductory course to learn how to speak "real" Spanish, but the idiom I encountered in the classroom didn't sound at all familiar. The first day of class, the teacher greeted me with "*¿Hola, qué tal?*," a phrase I'd never heard before. I blushed at my ignorance and stammered to reply, and the class went downhill from there. (I had learned to greet people with "*Buenos días,*" "*Buenas tardes,*" or "*Buenas noches.*" Some elders insisted on the even more formal "*le dé Dios*—may God grant you," as a coda to any greeting.) Also puzzling to me were the cultural trappings discussed in the class, such as the holidays. I hadn't heard of or celebrated Cinco de Mayo, Día de los

Muertos, or anyone's *quinceañera*. The Mexican hat dance? It was completely foreign to me. In any case, I would have been a laughing stock in Chimayó if I said, "*Hola*," and many other words and phrases taught in the class would have elicited the same kind of derision. The autochthonous variant of Spanish that we had become accustomed to in Chimayó was but one of many aspects of the culture that we learned to regard with more than a trace of embarrassment.

Still, in spite of all the obstacles to learning Spanish, the singsong New Mexico vernacular filled my ears when I visited Chimayó. Grownups lapsed into this mellifluous tongue to keep information from my siblings and me, which only heightened our attentiveness and unwitting comprehension. I learned scolding words first, since they were the most common ones directed at me: *zafado*, meaning silly, crazy, or just plain out of control; *malcriado*, meaning bad-mannered or rude; and *cabezudo*, which means headstrong or stubborn. We also learned simple greetings and niceties of social contact, as well as the abrupt commands that came our way ("*¡Cállate!*—Pipe down!" "*¡Vete!*—Get out of here!" "*¡Calla y come!*—Be quiet and eat!"), and we picked up more than a few *cochinadas* (obscenities) from the kids we ran with in Chimayó.

Also among the bits of language that stuck were short phrases that stood out because of their compactness or peculiar rhythm or rhyme. If I complained about food, Grandma might mutter, "*Con hambre no hay mal pan.*—When you're hungry, there is no bad-tasting food." To describe an exceedingly conceited person, she would say, "*Él piensa que nomás sus naranjas valen.*—He thinks only his oranges are worth something." If she disapproved of the companions I kept, Grandma might caution me, "*Él que con perros se acuesta con garrapatas se levanta.*—He who lies down with dogs wakes up with fleas." To be perfectly frank about her opinion of a character she disliked, she might say, "*Él no vale ni un cero a la izquierda.*—He's not even worth a zero to the left side" (referring to the left side of a multidigit number). When she overheard someone unfairly criticizing someone else, she was wont to say, "Oh, *ese hombre* has no place to talk. *Es como el burro hablando de orejas.*—It's like the burro talking about ears."

These old folk sayings, called "dichos" or "refranes," introduced me to a lot of language, and I carried a handful of them into adulthood.

Still more language seeped in through little songs Grandma would sometimes sing, two-line rhymes called *coplas*, longer verses (*versos*), and daily quips and exclamations of delight or dismay about events unfolding around her.

Then there were the *cuentos*, or folk tales (Mom and I gathered these together in a book, *Benigna's Chimayó: Cuentos from the Old Plaza*, published several years ago), prayers, and lullabies Grandma or Mom intoned at bedtime.

All in all, quite a lot of Spanish lodged in my memory even though the language seldom slipped from my tongue.

Since those formative years I've made countless visits to Chimayó and also lived there, next door to Grandma. In her final two decades, Grandma spoke only Spanish to me. She passed on in 2001 at the age of 103, and the last of her sisters and all the cousins of her generation have died since, leaving behind an empty space in the place and in our hearts. Every aspect of Chimayó has changed immensely. Although many people converse in a distinctive patois of English and Spanish, only a handful of monoglot Spanish speakers from the old families remain. Almost no one mentions the once-ubiquitous dichos that peppered all conversations with the viejitos.

As the years passed after Grandma's death, it dawned on me I could only remember a small fraction of her dichos, but I was mistaken when I assumed the rest had disappeared along with her and her generation of elders. My mother remembered many more than I could, and she had been writing them down since the early 1950s. Her list included nearly three hundred. In addition, Mom had saved a box of documents passed down to her through three centuries of our family's residency in Chimayó—a veritable treasure trove of language that could reveal much about the history of the Plaza del Cerro.

I was thrilled by the prospect of preserving and sharing this linguistic patrimony. My mother and I began translating and organizing the papers and the dichos. Suddenly, I found myself awash in the language of this singular place, Chimayó, and deep in the embrace of a tongue I was once forbidden to speak. As we worked with the words, Mom and I began to converse in Spanish. The language I had thought was nearly lost to me came back slowly as we delved into our task.

We also began taking more frequent trips to Chimayó, our newfound project providing us with an excuse to spend time together and visit old friends and family. Thus began a richly rewarding experience, a time to touch in with Chimayó people and places that had begun to grow distant. And as we drove through the valley and visited from house to house, the dichos and the language from the old documents ran through our heads and our conversations. It struck me how much the people and places I was visiting evoked the spirit of the dichos. I found them reflected everywhere within this old culture, in the language, the faces, the personalities, the conversation—all of it, like the dichos, seemingly poised on the edge of dissolution. And yet, the insight and wit and playfulness of the old sayings remain strong in the character of the place.

We immersed ourselves in the peculiar nuances of the Spanish, English, and Spanglish spoken in the valley. I learned new words and phrases and manners of expression, finding myself on a journey through the historic and contemporary language at the heart of the place. As my ability with the language grew, so too did my knowledge about neighborhoods away from the old plaza of my youth. I realized my experience of Chimayó growing up had been very sheltered and localized. I had rarely ventured far from Grandma's home by the Plaza del Cerro. This was partly because Grandma didn't have a car, but it was also because she warned us to stay away from places apart from the plaza. I'm sure this was motivated out of a desire to keep a close eye on us, but at the same time she made it clear that people from other parts of the valley were suspect. Grandma regarded the Plaza del Cerro as the bastion of good morals and respectable behavior. This was the family home of many generations, and she maintained a strong sense of cultural exclusivity about it, perhaps based on the plaza's status long ago as town center and home of Chimayó's *patrones*, or political bosses, many them from the Ortega side of her family.

My image of Chimayó apart from the familiar plaza also suffered from Chimayó's reputation in the outside world. Many of my peers in Los Alamos held Chimayó in low regard. I recalled the perspective I'd been exposed to in Los Alamos when I grew up, when "the Valley"—meaning the Hispanic and Pueblo communities along the Río Grande, below "the Hill" of Los Alamos—was the butt of condescending ethnic jokes and disparaging comments. Chimayó was generally regarded as a place of tragic cultural decline. Measured against the *Leave It to Beaver* social norms of the lofty Hill, Chimayó represented a backwater with little to offer.

This negative image did have some basis in fact. The viejitos cautioned us about the pachucos, a local term for ruffians or gangsters who cruised the highway and sometimes brawled nearby in the dark of night. Alcoholism and drug abuse plagued some families. Many of the kids my age in Chimayó regarded fighting not as an unacceptable behavior, but as a kind of daily sport and a rite of passage. I experienced this firsthand growing up as I was faced with no option but to go to fisticuffs with neighborhood kids. I emerged from these entanglements bruised and battered, but, paradoxically for me, I ended up being friends with my opponents. Others didn't fare so well, though, and we sometimes overheard or witnessed brutal fights that left people gravely injured. There always lingered in the back of my mind a real fear of being caught up in one of these events.

All the negative stereotypes about Chimayó and Hispanic culture in general weighed on me as I left the cocoon of the old plaza of my youth to explore Chimayó anew. From research for my master's thesis on Chimayó, I knew about the names and locations of other plazas in the Valley, and I had even lived for a short time away from the Plaza del Cerro, but I had rarely ventured into most of these foreign neighborhoods. Years of study of the Plaza del Cerro had impressed upon me that it was, indeed, the most formal plaza of the valley and was a center of political and economic life, but the nature of the other plazas remained a mystery to me.

Surprisingly, my mother also knew little about the broad Chimayó community. Her experience had also focused on the Plaza del Cerro of her youth. Even those parts of the valley she had visited as a child had changed so much they seemed new to her. Although she knew people here and there around Chimayó, she, too, was somewhat trepidatious as we encountered new places and people.

I began my explorations of the "other" plazas of Chimayó in 2008. When I go with my mother, we banter back and forth about the dichos. Talk fills our journeys to Chimayó. We jabber the full forty minutes it takes to get there and continue while we navigate the dirt roads in the valley and as we chat it up with relatives and friends there. Back home in Santa Fe, we call each other on the phone at all hours when we remember new dichos, and we wink at each other at family gatherings as we each recall dichos that apply to the situation at hand.

Shockingly to both of us, my mother is now considered a viejita herself (although she doesn't embrace the characterization at all!), and she tells me stories of the old days, just like Grandma once did. More unsettling still is the realization that I am next in line to hold and pass on this legacy. Our journeys are flavored with an acute sense of the poignancy of the transmission of thoughts, ideas, stories, and language—a chain stretching back for generations and now focusing on us during our day trips to the family *patria chica*.

Without exception, people in Chimayó receive us with warmth and kindness. Joy and amazement blossom on the faces of my mother's old friends and relatives when they greet us, but even "strangers" welcome us to their homes. Practically before we're in the door, the *plática* (conversation) begins—and in Chimayó, there's always plenty of talk to be had. They say talk is cheap, but I beg to differ. I've learned the cheap route would be breezing through Chimayó without stopping to check in with the *gente*, to reaffirm respect and affection for each other—and for life. It reminds me of how we used to go visiting in Chimayó when I was growing up, and the art of visiting is coming back to me. It's a dying art.

But Chimayosos indulge in the chitchat not just for nostalgia, nor is all of it trivial gossip. (In fact, whenever Mom notices that we're slipping into gossip, she'll stop and say, "*Cuidados ajenos matan al burro.*—Minding other people's business kills the donkey" or "*Cuida tu casa y deja la ajena.*—Mind your own house and leave others' alone.") The not-so-secret purpose of the plática is to weave together and keep intact a secure net of relationships. The conversation takes in a multitude of characters, many of them long gone but part of a community of memory that defines our place in the community of the living. The dead live among us, in our conversation, in the stories we tell. After all, in matters of the heart, time is not linear. We include in our plática the antepasados in the hope that we, too, will be remembered over coffee and bizcochitos one day.

What began as an effort to translate dichos has become a remarkable opportunity for making connections with family and new friends in Chimayó. Best of all, the endeavor has allowed my mother and me time together, engaged in an activity that has enriched our relationship in profound ways. At the same time, the experience has brought us a much deeper understanding of Chimayó, especially its older plazas and the viejitos who still inhabit them, even as the last vestiges of the old days slip away.

There are so many people we've visited with on this journey. Only a small number of those individuals and a fraction of the stories they told are recounted here. It's been a remarkable experience spending time with all of them as we delve deeply into this community we thought we knew but are actually discovering for the first time.

Magdalena Espinosa, La Cuchilla, 2009.

Esequiel and Magdalena in La Cuchilla

Para todo hay mañas, menos para la muerte.
There are tricks for everything—except for death.

Mom and I meet up at the De Vargas Mall in Santa Fe, where I transfer my camera gear to her car, and we head north, climbing out of Santa Fe and breaking the gravity of day-to-day routines to launch into the spacious northern New Mexico world. We have no idea where we'll go in Chimayó, but it doesn't matter. We're on our way and already feel ourselves entering a different temporal and spatial dimension.

It begins with the landscape, which works its alchemy well before arrival in Chimayó. The change starts along the fields of Nambé, where the car traffic slows from the frenetic pace on the main highway. The land secures its grip on our psyches and hearts in the empty spaces just beyond, where the open bowl of sky, rimmed by azure mountains, encircles a maze of barrancas and arroyos. The starkness, the silence, and the vast space—all these contribute to an exaggerated sense of distance and a corresponding stretching of time. The journey feels longer than the odometer tells us it is, the separation from the "other" world complete—and more than welcome.

We crest the top of arid barrancas and glide down the final hill into Chimayó, Mom pointing out the place where her late brother Robert Chávez's ashes are scattered, there where the view of the valley is best. It was his favorite vista, and, an artist by training and avocation, he painted this landscape more than once. Below us, to the east, we can just make out the old wagon road, mostly erased by a serpentine arroyo. My grandmother used to tell stories

Barrancas on the road to Chimayó, 2009.

about taking that road in a wagon loaded down with produce and blankets to sell in Santa Fe. Her trip to town involved an overnight campout by the Río Tesuque. Rolling into Santa Fe in predawn darkness (which presented her with her first glimpse of electric lights), she and her father, Reyes, would visit Jesusito "Sito" Candelario's Original Old Curio Store on San Francisco Street to sell the handwoven goods Reyes had made, then they'd set up by the plaza to sell melons, corn, and chile.

We make the trip in just over half an hour on this, the "new" road, completed forty-eight years ago, in 1965. Prior to the construction of the new road, we had to drive through Española to get to Chimayó, an entirely different journey following the verdant, long-settled Santa Cruz Valley, rather than the arid country past Nambé. This new route added to the trip the spectacular overview of Chimayó where we stop now to gaze out over the valley and remember Bobby, a much-loved child of this area—and one who did very well in the wider world, as a businessman in Albuquerque. My mother used to say about Bobby, quoting a dicho, "*Él que nace para guajes hasta jumates no para.*— One who is born to gourds won't stop until he becomes a dipper." (In other words, someone born to be great won't stop until he reaches the top.)

Mom also comments often about the work ethic that drove Bobby and his brother, Leo, to strive to make a better life for themselves outside of Chimayó. "They knew firsthand," says Mom, "that '*no hay bolsa más quieta que una bolsa sin dinero.*—there is no purse more still than a purse without money.' And so they worked hard—maybe too hard."

We continue downhill, around the big curve through Potrero, past the turnoff to the santuario, the church built by my great-great-great-great-grandfather, Bernardo Abeyta, and dedicated to El Señor de Esquipulas. The small adobe church, replete with impressive nineteenth-century paintings commissioned by Bernardo and executed by some of New Mexico's best artists, now draws tens of thousands of pilgrims and visitors each year. But we elect to skip the opportunity for healing earth. Ours is a pilgrimage of a different kind.

We cross the rushing Santa Cruz River, a vibrant ribbon of life that has always sustained the human communities in this place, including the small pueblos whose ruins remain amid cholla thickets on hilltops nearby. We cross on the "new bridge," as Grandma referred to it when she told of the days before there was an easy passage across the water. Then, she recalled, she used to cross the river by stepping cautiously on a series of chairs placed in the current by her father as he chaperoned her and her sisters to the dance hall in Potrero—an exciting adventure that took her a full mile away from her home.

Past the river, we glance over at the Rancho de Chimayó, the immensely popular restaurant that our cousin Arturo Jaramillo and his wife, Florence, opened right along the new road. They converted the home of his grandparents Hermenegildo and Trinidad Jaramillo (the daughter of my mother's great-aunt Epimenia Ortega Jaramillo) into a place whose appeal lay in the rural landscape, in the old building, and in the portraits of Arturo's family hanging on the walls. (My family and I attended the inaugural dinner at the Rancho. Amid the enthusiasm about Arturo and Flo's new venture, I remember hearing

Esequiel and Magdalena in La Cuchilla

whispers around tables that they had made a terrible miscalculation: nobody would make the tedious drive from Santa Fe across the empty badlands to visit a restaurant in an old adobe building in dusty old Chimayó. The naysayers were proved drastically wrong.)

We continue on, veering off the new highway to take the old road through the orchard that belonged to my grandmother's *comadre* Teresita Jaramillo, who was also her first cousin. The trees are withering and drying up, but I remember when they bore bumper crops of glowing red apples that Teresita and her husband, Severo, sold by the bushel. At one end of the orchard, we slow down by the small roadside shrine devoted to Danny Chávez, his smiling portrait and plastic flowers fading now. I remember the morning I came by here to find ribbons of police tape blocking off the orchard and a pool of dark red blood cupped by the fallen leaves beneath the trees, where Danny was gunned down.

It's barely a half mile from here to the Plaza del Cerro. We pull in through the east entrance to the plaza, past Eduardo Naranjo's store, long closed, where we used to buy candy as kids. We continue to the north side of the plaza, where I stop to take pictures of the windows and doors on the Cruz house. It's been a long downhill slide for the house since the old man, Pedro Cruz, died, and the adobe walls are deeply furrowed with cracks and are slowly melting away.

Motoring slowly around the plaza, we take care to avoid the rest of the north side, where a resident from nearby has posted Keep Out signs. He believes he owns the right-of-way, even though everyone knows it's long been a public pathway. In fact, we have a document affirming the primacy of this right-of-way, the *pisos de la plaza*, in 1848. Then, officials from Santa Cruz visited here and asked the oldest residents about customary rights-of-way on the plaza; the viejitos stated that there had always been a public path around the plaza, and the alcalde from Santa Cruz ruled that it should be respected and that no building or other encroachment would be tolerated.

Unfortunately, when the U.S. government surveyed properties in Chimayó in the early 1900s to legally confirm ownership under U.S. law, the public rights-of-way around the plaza were not included on maps. Neither were other important, long-recognized communal access ways to the ditches and the Santa Cruz River. Perhaps the current self-appointed guardian of the plaza and his few cronies rely on the map from the improper survey and ignore the deeper historical and customary precedents. In any case, for years he chased off tourists and locals alike in an attempt to guard a plaza—and a profound sense of history—that is slowly fading away.

This same person took me to task many times over the years I lived in Chimayó, because I was occasionally bringing people to see the plaza and because I argued for its preservation as a cultural treasure for Chimayó. I felt that I was educating people about a history I was proud of, which I regarded as a benefit to the community. But I learned the hard way that sometimes *"un bien con un mal se paga.*—a good deed is repaid with a bad one." After numerous encounters, in which he threatened me and shouted the same epithets I'd learned from local kids as a child, his confrontations with me culminated in a dark and brutal way: my beloved dog, Gerónimo, turned up beaten and battered and dying in front of our house. Although I never thought he was capable of doing such a thing, my nemesis jeered at me and declared that he was responsible for Gerónimo's mysterious and violent death. He intimated that he might just do the same to me.

The restraining order I obtained did little keep him from accosting me again in the plaza. One time I called the state police, and when they arrived on the scene to investigate, I recalled the advice a neighbor had given me—supposedly suggested to him by a law enforcement officer when the neighbor had similar troubles. At that time, the officer took him aside and counseled him in blunt and "strictly unofficial" terms: "Next time this guy bothers you, shoot him, make sure he's dead, and then drag him to your house." When my neighbor protested that this would land him in deep trouble, the uniformed officer handed him his business card and said, "I know how these guys operate. Call me. There won't be a problem."

As Mom and I talk about this local plaza vigilante and all the trouble he's brought to our family and to others, Mom reassures me, "Don't worry about it, 'jito, porque como dice el dicho, *'Nadie se va de este mundo sin pagar lo que debe.'*—like the saying goes, 'Nobody departs from this world without paying what he owes.'"

"*Y también*—and also," she continues, "'*No hay mal que por bien no venga.*—There is no evil that doesn't bring good."

Harrassment from this fellow and a few others has kept many people—even those with family roots in the plaza—from visiting or bringing guests there. And I can understand the sentiment that on some level motivates animosity toward visitors. A fear of the plaza becoming a tourist attraction or being taken over by "outsiders" fuels a determination among many in Chimayó to avoid the gentrification that has so altered Santa Fe and other Hispanic plaza towns. My argument that there is a way to preserve this singular place for its own and for the community's sake doesn't ease these fears. Unfortunately, as time goes on and people bicker about the plaza, entropy is winning. There is less to argue about every day.

Mom and I jog left at the west entrance to the plaza and drive down the west side, pausing in front of the chapel, known as the oratorio, its tilted belfry sadly empty.

"I can't believe they took the bell again," Mom laments, referring to the fact that the bell has recently been stolen—for the second time. A group of local people, including me, had labored long to fix the roof and replace the previous bell, ripped from the rooftop in the mid-1980s by thieves who at the same time made off with two priceless nineteenth-century bultos (carved wooden figurines) from inside the chapel.

"And remember when we dedicated the new bell?" Mom asks. "That was so nice." I do indeed recall the gathering on that cool fall day in 1995. Many former plaza residents stood here, in the field in front of the oratorio, to witness a blessing of the bell by the local priest, Father Roca (a celebrity in his own right). A feeling of joy swept through the group as we tolled the bell. Its tones, floating out over the weedy fields and neglected fruit trees of the disheveled plaza, seemed to rekindle, if only momentarily, a spirit of community that once lived here. Old women who'd prayed in the oratorio decades before stood on wavering legs amid the gathered crowd. When one of these viejitas, Teresita Jaramillo, went inside the chapel, she marveled she hadn't set foot in the oratorio for over forty years. Back then she sang hymns and prayed as one of the Carmelites, the laywomen's organization that cared for the chapel. Now she whispered and hummed to herself the old prayers.

Others in the group remembered the night in 1910 when the ringing bell woke them to stumble out and watch Halley's Comet light up the sky. In the predawn dark plaza residents had muttered in hushed tones, speculating on the portent of such an impressive cosmic display. So strong was the feeling of remembrance among the gathered crowd eighty-five years later that someone declared that this new bell must be the same one that had been stolen, returned to the oratorio by some miracle. But another resident said, "No, it doesn't sound quite like the old bell. I'll never forget that sound."

"It's too bad they stole the bell again," Mom repeats, wistfully. "And they did it in the middle of the night! '*Seguro que el diablo no duerme.*—It's true that the devil doesn't sleep.' It seemed for a while like we were going to bring people back to fix up the plaza."

To "fix up the old plaza" is a dream that has held some of us in its spell for many years (and has led to offers of funding by national foundations, an impressive moviemaker, and many others), but with each passing year the prospect seems farther away.

Mom and I don't have a key for the oratorio (it's kept safely by our cousins, who aren't in today) and so decide to travel on. We continue down the west side of the plaza, past rooms with their windows boarded, once the homes of Rafael and Perfecta Martínez, Isiderio and Pablita Ortega. We pause at the tiny room the viejitos called *el cuarto del Pancho*, with reference to its former resident Francisco (Pancho) Jaramillo. The roof on Pancho's humble abode has collapsed, the white window frames are splashed with mud, and trees grow freely inside the remnants of walls. Many of the plaza's buildings are facing the fate of Pancho's place, with the residents gone and the empty shells of their homes crumbling. But not all buildings have suffered this fate.

Around the south side, we pass the house where Antonio and Seferina Martínez lived, still well cared for and breathing life, thanks to the efforts of its new owner, Miguel da Silva. Just down the south side, the buildings that once housed the post office and general store, which used to belong to my grandma's Tío Victor, still stand; an old sign with simple hand lettering hangs on the white clapboard facade of the mercantile store: Post Office. But gone is the sign that hung here many years ago. That one, written in folksy handwritten script, read: *Victor D. J. Ortega: Comericante en Abarrotes y Efectos, Compra y Venda Productos del Pais*—Victor de Jesús Ortega: Merchant in Groceries and Goods, Buys and Sells Products of the Region. Victor, the plaza patrón, once ruled Chimayó with a firm Republican hand and held many important offices at the local, county, and state level. He reached what was perhaps the peak of his career when he served as a delegate to the New Mexico Constitutional Convention in 1910, but he never left his Chimayó roots. He remained a farmer and rancher as well as the local patrón until he died in 1944. (One neighbor from Potrero commented to me, "Victor, he was pretty sharp, but you knew he could be a really a big man here because '*en la ciudad de los ciegos el tuerto es rey.*—in the city of the blind the one-eyed man is king.'")

Esequiel and Magdalena in La Cuchilla

Now a bed-and-breakfast inn run by Jody Apple thrives in Victor's former residence.

We stop and tap the horn at Lorenzo Martínez's house, next to the old mercantile store. Lorenzo is the last plaza resident born and raised here. My grandmother was his *madrina* (godmother). Lorenzo leads a quiet existence in the home where his family has been for generations. We wait several minutes, but Lorenzo doesn't emerge.

FROM THE PLAZA DEL CERRO WE STRIKE OUT, AWAY FROM OUR FAMILIAR haunts. We cross the Cañada Ancha arroyo and climb into sandy hills toward the Plaza de Nuestra Señora del Carmen, also known as La Cuchilla. Our spontaneous intention is to seek out an old friend, Magdalena Espinosa, who lives next door to her daughter Josie Luján, just off La Cuchilla plaza. We haven't seen Magdalena since she came to Grandma's one hundredth birthday party, ten years ago.

As we drive through the vestiges of the original La Cuchilla plaza, we pass the chapel dedicated to Nuestra Señora del Carmen (Our Lady of Mount Carmel), a Madonna with her origin in the Old World in the fifteenth century. If there was a formal plaza here, its rectangular layout is no longer apparent. The chapel is just about the only feature remaining to identify the plaza, whose name first appears on our family documents in 1837 in the last will and testament of José Antonio Cruz, *"residente de la plasa de mi señora del Carmen—* resident of the plaza of My Lady of Mount Carmel." My great-great-great-grandfather, Gervacio Ortega, served as an albacea (executor) of the will. Writing in 1837, Cruz leaves 757 varas of land, two houses, some fruit trees, a hoe, and an ax to his daughter, María Manuela. He leaves another small house to *"mi padre mio San Juaquin,"* his patron saint. Exactly where those houses stood we'll probably never know.

We negotiate the final tight turns in La Cuchilla, through a warren of houses and trailers on small lots that divide up once-productive farmland, to reach Magdalena's well-kept adobe house. It's all locked up and quiet, but we know she doesn't leave home much these days, so I knock and then knock again. Finally I hear a voice and then notice a figure in the darkness, approaching the door. To my surprise I see the wide smile of Esequiel Trujillo through the steel security door. He swings the door open wide. "*¡Pase!*— Come in!"

I met Esequiel on a few occasions when I lived in Chimayó. Esequiel is best known as a nimble Matachín dancer. He is charismatic, friendly, and talkative, and he cuts a striking figure: tall, slender, high jawboned, with ample eyebrows leaning over light-blue eyes. He usually wears a black broad-brimmed hat that lends an air of rustic formality to his attire. He's fit for his eighty-plus years. His knowledge of and passion for telling old stories about Chimayó, conveyed in a high-pitched, melodic Spanish, impressed me over the years in animated conversations we had during chance meetings in the post office, and I've always wanted to talk with him at greater length.

Esequiel is hatless today and wears a button-down blue shirt. He also has glasses on. He tells me he is taking care of his cousin Magdalena for the day. It seems at first a bit odd that an eighty-year-old is caring for a ninety-nine-year-old, but Esequiel appears perfectly capable and glad to be spending time with his prima.

Mom and I enter the dimly lit, warm interior of the house. Magdalena, in a lavender dress, is seated on a couch in the sala. She peers at us with a penetrating gaze through classic '50s-era horned-rim glasses. She's bright and alert and remembers us clearly.

Esequiel and Magdalena look like they're ready for church, but they're just passing the time together, cousins in their twilight years alone in a quiet corner of Chimayó. Esequiel leads my mother to sit on the couch beside Magdalena, offers me a stuffed chair, and pulls a wooden one from the kitchen for himself. The stage is set for the polite and warm plática to follow, all of it in the peculiar old Spanish I remember hearing as a child. I feel a familiar sense of time suspended.

Magdalena begins by addressing my mother, "*O, yo quería mucho a su mamá, y ella quería mucho a mí.*—Oh, I loved your mother so much, and she loved me." She reminds us Grandma was her grade school teacher around 1920 in the tiny, one-room adobe schoolhouse in La Cuchilla.

"*Sí, venía a pie cada día para La Cuchilla para enseñar a los niños.*—Yes, she walked every day to La Cuchilla to teach the kids," Magdalena says in her deep, husky voice. "*Era muy buena maestra y muy buena conmigo.*—She was a very good teacher and very good to me."

After a few minutes of silence, we turn to a discussion of the Matachines dances. Although Spanish colonists developed its formal choreography, this dance drama has its roots in medieval Spain. Both Native and Hispanic villages perform it, from northern New Mexico southward through Mexico. Each dance group expresses the story differently, but it's most often interpreted as a battle of good versus evil, played out by several characters.

Esequiel led Matachines performances for some years in Chimayó. I ask how he learned the dance, and he comes alive, answering in a voice as scratchy and vibrant as an old violin.

"*Aprendí de mi papá, y él aprendió de un indio de San Juan que era gobernador.*—I learned from my father, and he learned from an Indian who was the governor of San Juan Pueblo," he says. "*Mi papá, él se crió con los indios en el pueblo, y trabajaba allí mucho con los indios.*—My father, he grew up there with the Indians in the pueblo, and he worked there a lot with the Indians."

"*Y le dijo el gobernador, 'Nunca dejes tu danza, nadie te la quita, ésta es tuya en Chimayó. Lo mismo que aquí en el pueblo.'*—And the governor told him, 'Never forget your dance. No one can take it from you. This is your dance, in Chimayó, the same as here in the pueblo.'"

Esequiel goes into detail explaining the intricacies of the Matachines performance. He tells of the *monarca* (king), who wears a corona (crown); the young girl or princess named Malinche, who is dressed in virginal white; a toro (bull); two clowns or *abuelos* (grandfathers); and several *danzantes* (dancers) who are sometimes referred to as soldiers or warriors.

"*Todos los danzantes, menos la Malinche, traen máscaras.*—All the dancers except Malinche wear masks," he says. "*Y el monarca trae una palma y un guaje, y músicos tocan violín y guitarra.*—And the king carries a trident and a gourd, and musicians play a guitar and violin.

"*Yo era el líder de la danza, aquí en Chimayó. Una vez fuimos pa' Santa Fe, allá en un museo. Y me preguntaron la gente, '¿Cómo sabe usted bailar?' Y les dije, 'La educación que tengo, lo traigo aquí, en esta cabeza.*—I was the leader of the dance here in Chimayó," he continues. "One time we went to Santa Fe, to dance at the museum there. And the people asked me, 'How do you know how to dance?' And I told them, 'I carry it here, in this cabeza.'" (He points to his head.) "*Allí en el santuario bailamos también. Todos los años bailamos el día primero del año.*—There at the santuario we danced, too. Every year we danced on the first of January," he reminisces, letting out a hearty laugh at the memory. Then he turns serious and sighs heavily, recalling the death of his nephew, whom he had hoped would take over as the lead dancer.

"*Sí, Dios sabe toda la tragedia, pero ya no quiero yo andar allí. Si yo voy andar con ellos, dirigiendo, pero ya no—mover en la danza, ¿no?*—Yes, God knows the whole tragedy, but I don't want to go there. Yes, I'll go with the dancers, but no longer will I move in the dance, you know?

"*Pero yo tengo todo el equipaje para la danza. Todas las coronas y vestidos. La ropa está allá en la petaquilla. Tengo el equipaje. Y luego el vestido de los abuelos. Lo compuse de sacos de guangoche, los en que venden papas. Y lo compuse bien todo, el chaleco, las máscaras, . . . nomás por no conocer quién es el abuelo.*—But I have all the stuff for the dance. All the crowns and outfits. It's all there in the wooden chest. And the costumes for the abuelos. I made them out of burlap potato sacks. I put all that stuff together, the vest, the masks . . . just so no one will know who it is dancing as the abuelos."

Animated again, Esequiel bursts into laughter.

"*Yo animé a mi familia, como me animó my papá. Que no dejara a la cultura.*—I inspired my family to dance, just like my father inspired me. I told them not to leave behind their culture," he continues. "*Y mi sobrina que está en Seattle, Washington, ahora viene pa' Crismes. Y tengo parte de la familia en Denver, el modo es que van a venir p'acá para hacer la danza. Van a bailar allá al santuario o aquí a la iglesia, o tal vez bailan aquí en casa, yo no sé.*—And my niece who is in Seattle, Washington, she's coming now, for Christmas. Part of my family is also in Denver, so they're coming here to do the dance. They'll dance at the santuario, or at the church, or maybe at my house. I don't know."

I inquire if anyone had performed the Matachines in Chimayó before he brought it back.

Turning to his elder cousin, Magdalena, Esequiel inquires, "*Bailaban allí en La Cuchilla antes, ¿qué no, prima?*—They danced there in La Cuchilla before, didn't they, prima?"

Magdalena nods. "*Sí. En La Cuchilla. Y era muy bonito! También en la capilla allá abajo, la que está al lado de la iglesia grande—allí bailaban cuando tenían funciones. El día veintiocho, Los Inocentes, allí bailaban. Y había mucha gente en aquellos tiempos.*—Yes, in La Cuchilla, and it was really nice. And also in the chapel down below, the Plaza de Abajo, there by the new, big church—they danced there for feast days, like the twenty-eighth of December, the Day of the Holy Innocents. They danced there. There were many people in those days," Magdalena answers.

"*Benigno me curó de este pie.*—Benigno fixed this leg," Magdalena says, changing the subject to Esequiel's father, who taught him the dance. "*No podía andar. Andaba en la wheelchair. Me caí y me lo quebré. Y me curó.*—I couldn't walk. I was in a wheelchair. I fell and broke the leg. And he healed me."

"*Su papá era don Benigno?*—Your father was Don Benigno?" my mother exclaims. "*¿Benigno era muy buen sobador.*—He was a really good *sobador*," she says. I, too, recall the old man, Don Benigno, a renowned massage therapist, chiropractor, and herbalist all in one, who sometimes came to work on my grandmother's injured knee. "*Todos le tenían mucha fe a don Benigno.*—Everyone had faith in Don Benigno," Mom states unequivocally. "*Era uno de los últimos curanderos aquí.*—He was one of the last healers in the area."

Esequiel nods: "*Fue hasta Chromo y Leadville a curar a los que lastimaban en las minas. Hasta Denver fue. Y les preguntó a la gente allí, '¿Qué no tienen buenos doctores aquí en Denver?' Y dijeron que sí habían, pero no sabían curar.*—He went as far as Chromo and Leadville in Colorado, to heal men who were hurt in the mines. All the way to Denver, he went, and he would ask the people there, 'Don't you have good doctors here in Denver?' And they would tell him yes, there were doctors, but they didn't know how to heal."

Noticing a portrait of a couple on the table behind Magdalena, I ask who the people are.

"*Éste es me papá, Valentín Trujillo, y mi mamá, que se llamaba Celsa Chávez.*—This is my father, Valentín Trujillo, and my mother, who was called Celsa Chávez."

"*O, era Chávez?*—Oh, she was a Chávez?" Mom asks. "*Yo también.*—So am I."

"*Pero no era de aquí, ella. Era de San Pablo, Colorado.*—But my mother wasn't from here. She was from San Pablo, Colorado."

"*Mi papá también era de Colorado.*—My father was from Colorado, too," Mom responds.

"*Yo conocí a tu papá, don Reyes.*—I knew your father, Don Reyes," Magdalena says.

"*No, mi papá se llamaba Abedón, de los Chávez aquí en Potrero.*—No, my father was Abedón, of the Chávezes here in Potrero," Mom replies.

"*O, sí. Lo conocí también. Tu abuelito era Reyes Ortega.*—Oh, of course," Magdalena says. "I knew him, too. Your grandfather was Reyes Ortega."

"*Papá mencionaba mucho a los Ortegas.*—My father talked a lot about the

Ortegas," Esequiel offers. "*Era muy amigable a ellos.*—He was very friendly with them."

Changing the subject suddenly again, Magdalena asks Esequiel, "*¿Cuánto tiempo desde murió mi hermanito?*—How long has it been since my brother died?"

"*Dos meses.*—Two months," he answers. "*Ya dos meses desde murió Abel del derrame. Tenía noventa y dos años. Y mi hermano Lionicio murió el año pasado a los noventa y tres años, de cáncer.*—Already two months since Abel died of that stroke! He was ninety-two. And my brother Lionicio died last year at ninety-three, of cancer."

A long silence fills the room, until Magdalena offers, "*Yo tenía siete años nomás cuando murió mi mamá.*—I was only seven years old when my mother died."

"*¿Y quedó huérfana?*—You were left an orphan?" Mom asks.

"*Sí, y mi hermanito Abel tenía nomás que dos años.*—Yes, and my little brother, Abel, was only two years old."

"*¿Quién los cuidaba?*—Who took care of you?" my mother asks.

Magdalena points to her chest and nods firmly, proudly: "*Yo me cuidé sola. Y crié a mi hermanito.*—I took care of myself. And I raised my little brother."

"*¿A los siete años?*—When you were seven years old?" Mom asks, incredulously.

"*Sí, y Abel y no nunca estábamos apartes, ¿qué no, primo?*—Yes, and Abel and I were never apart, right, primo?" Magdalena asks, turning to Esequiel, who nods.

"*Nunca.*—Never," she says again and looks down at the floor.

"*¿Y cuándo murió su cuñada Pilar?*—And when did your sister-in-law Pilar die?" I ask, remembering the wonderful, warm viejita who lived next door to Magdalena.

"*No me acuerdo—pero espérate. Yo te digo.*—I don't remember—but wait, I'll tell you," she says, furrowing her brow and looking up at the ceiling. "*Tres años.*—Three years."

"*Y mi primo José y su esposa, ¿ya habían muerto antes de Pilar, qué no?*—And my cousin José and his wife, they had already died before Pilar, right?" Esequiel asks.

"*O, seguro. Muchos años antes. Y Pilar ya tenía . . .* Oh, certainly. That was many years before. And Pilar was almost . . ." Magdalena replies, looking

Esequiel and Magdalena in La Cuchilla 27

again at the ceiling, "*Tenía casi ciento cinco cuando murió.*—She was almost 105 when she died."

"*¿¡Ciento cinco!?*—One hundred and five!?" says Esequiel.

"*Mi mamá mía tenía ciento tres.*—My mother was 103," Mom adds.

"*Yo la quería mucho.*—I loved her very much," Magdalena says again. "*Y ella me quería a mí.*—And she loved me."

"*¡Mire no más!*—My word!" Esequiel adds. "*¡Fíjese!*—Just imagine."

"*Sí, fíjese.*—Yes, just imagine," Mom says, and there follows another long silence.

DICHOS ABOUT MORTALITY

Achaque busca la muerte para llevarse al difunto.
   Death looks for excuses to take the deceased away. (Don't give death any excuses.)

El muerto al pozo y el vivo al retozo.
   The dead to the grave and the living to the frolic. (Said sarcastically when a spouse dies and the surviving partner starts having a good time right away.)

Él que por su gusto muere, hasta la muerte le sabe.
   To a person who dies for his own pleasure, even death tastes good. (Said of someone who does foolhardy or dangerous things, knowing full well the consequences.)

Nadie se lleva lo que tiene.
   Nobody takes with him what he owns. (Nobody takes his worldly goods with him when he dies.)

Para todo hay mañas, menos para la muerte.
   There are tricks for everything—except for death. (All problems have solutions except for death.)

Nadie se va de este mundo sin pagar lo que debe.
   Nobody departs from this world without paying what she owes. (Debts and obligations always catch up to you.)

Parece la muerte en calzoncillos.
   He looks like death wearing underpants. (He looks like death warmed over.)

Tomasita, 2011.

Tomasita's Chile Colorado from the Plaza de Abajo

Vale más amigos que dinero en el banco.
Friends are worth more than money in the bank.

My mother and I make a special trip to Chimayó every fall, not to gather holy dirt at the famed santuario, but for something almost equally revered: Chimayó chile.

We've always relied on Chimayó friends and relatives to grow chile for us, since we don't have farmland. In fact, our immediate family was separated from the land quite a while back, and we lost our self-sufficiency in chile. The separation began when my great-grandfather, Reyes Ortega, opened a weaving shop in Chimayó (he was the first to do so) and spent more time weaving and less in his extensive farmland in Chimayó and Truchas. Reyes continued to grow chile for his family's consumption, though, and I have seeds from his plants. But when Grandma acquired land from him above the Acequia de los Ortegas and built her home there, she didn't have access to irrigation water. Her three children didn't grow up farming, although most of their neighbors and relatives did. (Grandma's family did haul all their domestic water, including drinking water, in buckets uphill from the ditch.) Still, they all acquired a taste—you might say an addiction—for the homegrown chile from Chimayó.

Precious few in number are the farmers who still grow the old, "native" Chimayó varieties of chile. These small, crooked, but extremely flavorful chiles were decades ago supplanted in mainstream markets by hybridized varieties that are bigger, meatier—and, in my judgment, far less flavorful. Back in the first half of the twentieth century, chile from northern New Mexico dominated the national chile trade, but growers in Chimayó couldn't compete when agricultural interests in southern New Mexico and in other states took up mechanized chile farming on a large scale. As has happened with much produce, by sheer economies of scale the big growers began to depress prices and to determine tastes at the consumer level. Chimayó chile was all but forgotten for some time.

Most Chimayó growers kept *huertas* of chile near their homes, even if they no longer grew chile for cash. They still do. We're fortunate to have connections to some of these elite growers. For many years, our source was Sofía Trujillo in Rincón de los Trujillos, a Chimayó neighborhood not far from the Plaza del Cerro. Sofía's husband, Genaro, was a son of Grandma's Tía Senaida. This made Genaro Grandma's primo and Sofía, her prima. Since Sofía was also a dear friend, she was under a certain obligation to offer us chile. But prima Sofía stopped growing chile years ago and has now passed on. For the past decade we've relied upon Tomasita. (I don't give her full name because, with locally grown chile so scarce, I don't want to reveal our current source.)

So, as we do every fall, we're making our pilgrimage for chile. We turn on State Road 76 toward Española and pass by Trujillo's Weaving Shop, a fine establishment set up by Grandma's cousin Johnny Trujillo. We manage to resist the temptation (mine only) to stop in at the Chile Red Tavern, the only local bar in Chimayó, and we sail on down the highway, commenting here and there on familiar homes and landmarks: the ruins of Moose's Bar, now just a pile of crumbled adobes; the roadside *descanso* for Tommy Martínez, killed at the spot over a drug deal gone bad; Orlando's general store, the last of its kind in town (Orlando's grandmother was my grandmother's first cousin, so he's another primo to call on now and then). After the *estafeta* or post office and the Holy Family Church, we turn up "Tomasita's arroyo," as we call it.

The general neighborhood here is anchored by a local chapel, La Capilla de Nuestra Señora de los Dolores. In deference to this old capilla, this part of Chimayó is often called the Plaza de Dolores, although there is no recognizable plaza anymore. The neighborhood is also referred to as Plaza de Abajo, the Plaza Below. The Dolores chapel is similar in size to the several others in the valley, from Santa Cruz all the way to Potrero—perhaps a dozen in all, each dedicated to its own *santo patrón* (patron saint). For most of the valley's history, these chapels served the religious needs of extended families or small neighborhoods, since the nearest official branch of the Catholic Church was in Santa Cruz de la Cañada, ten miles down the road—a long haul, in the days of horse and wagon. The Holy Family Church and Parish were designated in Chimayó in the 1960s, just across the road from the Dolores chapel.

Visitors to Chimayó assume the santuario is the primary Catholic church in Chimayó and the seat of the local parish, since it is the focus of the famous pilgrimage and the destination for most tourists coming to Chimayó. But the santuario was for many decades just another of these neighborhood chapels, albeit the largest. (In fact, it belonged to my ancestors in the Chávez line, descendants of Bernardo Abeyta, the founder of the church.) This misconception irked our late cousin Modesto Vigil so much that he often made it a point on Good Friday to walk against the flow of the pilgrim traffic, away from the santuario toward the Holy Family Church, excoriating the pilgrims. "You're going the wrong way!" he would shout at the thousands of walkers streaming along the highway. "The sacraments are in the other church, not the santuario!" He was correct, of course; the santuario is but a mission administered from the parish center a few miles down the road. But his single-handed crusade was in vain.

Few drivers on Highway 76 even notice the lovely white capilla dedicated to the Señora de los Dolores, standing in an apple orchard across the highway from the new church. We pass it by, too, as we hurry along and turn up Tomasita's arroyo and into her driveway. Tomasita comes out of her house to welcome us. I can feel myself slowing down to Chimayó time again as she walks toward us, waving and smiling.

It's not for the money that Tomasita grows chile. And it's not just for the chile that we come to visit her. Now in her late seventies, Tomasita works hard taking care of the finicky plants through the heat of summer. She did this almost single-handedly for years while her husband worked away in Los Alamos. He's gone now, and her kids are busy working most of the time. That leaves Tomasita alone in the huerta more often than not.

The art of raising chiles came to Tomasita through her father, Fidel Coriz, who planted his chile in the nearby plaza of La Cuchilla. In those days, Tomasita and her family had to work the chile well into the fall, tying *ristras* that her father would take to the Bond and Nohl store in Española to exchange for much-needed cash or for goods. It *was* for the money, then. Tens of thousands of ristras shipped out each year from Española on the railroad called, appropriately enough, the Chile Line (or, more formally, the Denver & Río Grande Western).

Chile ristras have been valued as trade items in New Mexico for a long time. One of our family papers, written in 1850, mentions two chile ristras, along with a long list of other items, as payment for the funeral Mass of María Pascuala Romero, my great-great-great-grandfather's mother-in-law.

Now Tomasita admits she sometimes wonders why she labors away at growing chile, especially when the Acequia del Distrito (the "District Ditch," the large ditch that comes from the Santa Cruz Irrigation District dam) is dry and the plants are thirsty, or when the weeds are thick and there's no one to help hoe them. There's a young child in the house, too, Tomasita's grandson, for whom she cares while her daughter is away working. Between the child and the chiles and recovering from the recent loss of her husband, Tomasita seems a bit worn as she calls out the customary Chimayó greeting, "Get down!"—meaning to get out of the car and come in for a sit in the sala (salon or living room) of her house. It's a ritual that happens in just about every visit to Chimayó. We simply must take the time to relax and partake in the plática. It's about checking in with the gente, I'm reminded again.

Warm embraces all around are followed with "*¿Cómo ha estado?*—How have you been?" and "Oh, pretty good," followed by a general health report. Then Tomasita says, "*Pasen, pasen.*—Come in, come in."

I'm anxious to learn the family connections, so I ask. I'm amazed at the answer that spills out, from both Mom and Tomasita, a tangle of names and relationships that leaves me dizzy.

"It goes back to Severo Martínez," Mom says, "who married Leonides Ortega's daughter; Leonides was your great-grandpa Reyes's sister. Leonides's daughter died and left a baby girl named Fidelita. Then Severo married another of Leonides's daughters, named Julianita. So he married two sisters, see?"

I don't see, even though I've had all this explained to me before. But Tomasita picks up the thread: "Severo's parents were Epifanio and María de los Ángeles Martínez. Besides Severo they had Petrita, Sabina, Faustina, and Cayetano. Petrita had Bernardita, my mother, as well as Evangelia, Pula, Manuel, Ascensión, and Juliana. Therefore Petrita was Fidelita's aunt, Bernardita's first cousin, and my second cousin."

"But none of these had Ortega blood, except for Fidelita," Mom points out, "because she was Leonides's granddaughter. Severo by his second wife, Julianita, had Pulita, Seledón, Antonio, Oralia, and Susie. I think there was another girl between Oralia and Susie. Leonides had Francisco, Miguel, Romana, and

Gregoria, besides the one that died and Julianita. Gregorita's husband's name was Eugenio; they were Orlando's parents."

"I knew Gregorita, and of course I know Orlandito," I interject, using the diminutive form of Orlando, as my grandmother used to refer to him. "Gregorita was Grandma's cousin. But I still don't see how she was related to Tomasita."

"She wasn't, really. Tomasita's grandmother, Petrita, was a sister-in-law to Gregorita's mother, Julianita. So Tomasita's mother was Gregorita's cousin, through marriage."

"So we're not related, really?" I ask.

"No, but we're primos!" Mom and Tomasita laugh.

I'm totally dumbfounded that these women can remember so many names and connections, and I'm ready to move on to the chile.

Tomasita has two houses: one where she lives and one where she processes and stores her chile. She and her husband built the smaller "chile house" by themselves soon after they were married, and they later built the house where she now lives. Both places have salas apportioned with soft sofas and easy chairs, with rows of family photos and religious images on the walls. I get the feeling the chile house has become a kind of refuge for Tomasita.

We enter the sala in the chile house. It's late fall and very cool inside, since the place is unheated to keep the chile fresh. It reeks of chile peppers—an old, familiar, and intoxicating fragrance that stirs nostalgia—and puts us in the mood for buying and eating chile.

We sit, and the conversation continues, in Spanish then English then back, about the weather, the family, with always kind words of remembrance about my grandmother, who was very close to Tomasita's mother, Bernardita—hence the privilege of getting to buy the cleanest, brightest, most pungent and flavorful red chile powder I've ever seen. But we don't mention chile at all at first; it would be impolite to rush to the transaction. (As Mom says when I try to rush past formalities like this, "*¡Quieres pasar la acequia antes de llegar a la puente!*— You want to cross the ditch before you get to the bridge!") We've come for the talk, for the reconnection, to check up on each other, as much as for the magical substance as red as blood that will consummate our friendship.

Eventually we've touched on all the important topics, covered all the recent deaths and illnesses, lamented all the terrible losses and celebrated all the new gains (like Tomasita's darling but very demanding grandchild). We finally turn to the chile—and the news, at first, is not good. We've come late in the season, and Tomasita has sold out all her chile, not to mention the few dozen ristras she tied. I try not to look disappointed.

But then Tomasita brightens and says, "I'll sell you some of mine," suggesting the nearly unthinkable possibility she would break into her own stash for us. "Oh no," Mom protests, "We don't want you to do that."

"*No te acongojes*—Don't worry," Tomasita insists. "Anyway, I kept a few extra pounds, just in case." As she leads us to the back room, I imagine it's something like entering a private wine cellar in Provence.

Tomasita reaches into a box and extracts four or five one-pound baggies of chile powder while my mother continues to protest and I scowl at her to stop resisting.

"Will this be enough?" Tomasita asks.

"Of course, of course," Mom replies, graciously accepting at last.

"Do you like chile *caribe*?" Tomasita asks me as she surveys the stores in her fragrant chile hoard, looking for something to gift us.

"I love it," I blurt out, unable to hide my greed at the prospect of getting hold of this special grind of chile. (Mom gives me a look that says, "*Te ofrece almohada y quieres colchón.*—She offers you a pillow and you want a mattress," a dicho that is roughly equivalent to "She gives you an inch and you want a mile.") Chile caribe looks like the flakes that come in shakers on tables in Italian restaurants; it's made by grinding up dried pods very loosely, rather than taking them to the mill for a fine grinding. Grandma simply used to crumple chiles in her hands or crush them with a pastry roller to make caribe. Caribe has a tangy, sharp flavor distinct from the taste of the fine-ground chile powder, even though both grinds of chile come from the same pods.

Everyone has their special chile obsession. For some it's fresh green. For others, it's caribe. For me, it's Tomasita's red chile *molido* (ground red). Still, caribe is a special treat, not to be passed up. It reminds me of mornings with Grandma, who often fixed chile caribe with eggs and *papas* for breakfast. Tomasita says, "I'll just give you this," handing me a plump pound of chile caribe.

Before our transaction with Tomasita can be consummated, we have a final ritual to perform. I open a baggy of the chile molido and stick in a moistened finger, then transfer the pinch of crimson powder to my tongue. A sweet sharpness floods my mouth and relays into my nasal passages and then down my throat, leaving a satisfying, lingering warmth. It's fresh, pure, real—not that I ever doubted that it would be. Tomasita roasted and then cleaned each pod by hand, removing every seed and bit of stem or leaf. She took her harvest to the miller in Río Chiquito and saw to it that the pods were ground to just the right consistency.

Mom repeats the finger-dunking ritual. The product of Tomasita's labors is coursing through our systems like fiery tracers in a dark sky. This is satisfaction. After *abrazos* all around, we place the comfortingly hefty bags in our car and head back toward Santa Fe.

DICHOS ABOUT FRIENDSHIP AND ENMITY

Cada oveja con su pareja.
   Each sheep with its partner. (Everyone has a like-minded friend.)

Cuídame de mis amigos que de mis enemigos yo me cuidaré.
   Protect me from my friends, for I will protect myself from my enemies. (Some friends are worse than enemies.)

Dádivas quiebran peñas.
   Gifts break rocks. (You can break down a person's animosity with gifts.)

Dime con quién andas y yo te diré quién eres.
   Tell me who you hang around with, and I'll tell you who you are. (You are known by the company you keep.)

El más amigo es traidor.
   The friendliest one is a traitor. (Beware of overly friendly people.)

Él que a buen árbol se arrima, buena pedrada le dan.
   He who moves close to a good tree gets hit hard. (Said of one who tries to get in with people of higher class and is painfully snubbed.)

Esos son desaires que se agradecen.
   That is a snub that is welcomed. (You did me a favor by rebuffing me.)

Más moscas se cazan con miel que con vinagre.
   More flies are caught with honey than with vinegar.

Nadie puede obligar a quien lo quieran.
>   You can't force anyone to like you.

No le debo ni los buenos días.
>   I don't even owe him a "Good morning." (The time for civility has passed.)

No quiere al indio pero el guayabe, sí.
>   He might not like the Indian, but he likes the piki bread the Indian makes. (Said of someone who doesn't want anything to do with a person, but will gladly take what the person has to offer.)

Que se empine pa' el Norte pa' que le caiga la nieve de golpe.
>   Let him bend to the north so the snow will hit him with full force. (Stubbornness is rewarded with consequences.)

Vale más amigos que dinero en el banco.
>   Friends are worth more than money in the bank.

Vale más solo que mal acompañado.
>   Better to be alone than with bad companions.

Vale más un vecino cerca que pariente lejos.
>   It is better to have a neighbor nearby than a relative far away.

Lorenzo Martinez, Plaza del Cerro, 2008.

Lorencito in the Plaza del Cerro

Nomás él que carga el costal sabe lo que trae adentro.
Only the one who carries the sack knows what is inside.

Today I'm on my own, and I elect to stay close to the Plaza del Cerro. It's unusually warm for late October in Chimayó, but the cottonwoods along Acequia del Distrito, the ditch that traverses the plaza, are brilliant with fall color. A beaver has taken up residence, and several trees lie prone on the ground, victims of the creature's busyness. His prospects for survival are slim, since his work is sure to interfere with ditch operations and will not be tolerated. Still, I'm rooting for him. The trees he is felling are mostly invasive, nonnative Siberian elms that have overrun the plaza. Furthermore, I view the ditch he has colonized as an alien intrusion, since it is not the historic water source for the plaza. That small ditch, the Acequia de los Ortegas, is much humbler in stature and would never accommodate a beaver. The new ditch, called the District Ditch, the Acequia del Distrito, or the Acequia del Depósito (the Ditch from the Dam), was dug through here when the Santa Cruz Dam was built in 1929, against the wishes of the plaza residents. None of them have rights to water from this glutton of a ditch. On the other hand, its water nurtures the chiles I buy from Tomasita, a few miles downstream; she might not have water in the late summer were it not for the dam.

I cross the plaza from east to west along the road and turn south to motor slowly by the decrepit but marvelously evocative buildings along the western side. I recall a winter day when I was photographing this side of the plaza, just after a fresh snowfall. In the early dawn light, I was shooting with a large-format camera on a tripod, my head covered with a dark cloth. I heard a car slip into the plaza, its loose muffler's rumble dampened by the new snow. The car stopped close by, and I heard the door open and footsteps coming toward me. Startled, I emerged from the darkness of the black cloth, and the inverted image of the old plaza lingered in my vision against the white snow. As my eyes adjusted to the brightness, I saw a man standing in front of me. He was very drunk and swaying uncertainly. He was not from my neighborhood.

"What you doing?" he asked. I told him I was taking photographs. He looked toward the old buildings that my camera was pointed at and shook his head. "Of that?" he asked, incredulous. I explained that I thought the old buildings were really beautiful with the new snow.

"How much did that camera cost?" he asked. I told him that it had been a gift to me, but he didn't believe me. His eyes narrowed as he sized me up. The driver in the car started to laugh. I began to think this little scenario could end badly. The teetering drunk in front of me glanced up and down the road and around the abandoned plaza. There was no one around.

"Why don't you give me twenty bucks?" he said.

"I don't have any money on me," I said. "I live up the road and I just walked down here."

"How about ten bucks?"

"I don't have have even ten cents."

"You from here?" he asked. I told him of my family connections, but he wasn't from the plaza and didn't seem to know any names.

"You can just give me that camera and we'll let it go at that," he said. I laughed and thought, "*Me quiere jugar un dos por cuatro.*—He wants to give me two for four." (Meaning he wants to cheat me.) I explained to him said that this was a very old camera that no one would want and hardly anyone would know how to use. My levity seemed to unsettle him, and it was he who now became suspicious. I could imagine him thinking, "*Me quiere tapar el sol con la mano.* He wants to cover the sun with his hand." (He wants to make a fool out of me.) He looked back in the car at the waiting driver, who seemed to have fallen asleep at the wheel, his head lolling loosely, then scowled at me.

"Just hand me the f——ing camera," he said.

"No way."

He paused a minute, then said, "Eeee, you're a trip, man! A real trip." And he got in the car and nudged the driver, who snapped awake and drove them away.

I told my grandmother about the encounter when I arrived back home that early morning to sit and have some breakfast of atole with her. She frowned at the mention of the man's name and said, "*O, ese hombre. Tiene más entradas que salidas.*—He has more entries than exits," a dicho that she liked to use for someone who thinks he is very smart, but isn't. "*También*—also," she went on, "*no vale ni un cero a la izquierda.*—he's not worth even a zero to the left side!"

The fellow who had accosted me that day died of a drug overdose a year or two later. Thankfully, today I find someone much friendlier in the plaza, framed by the doorway of the chapel: one of the Trujillo twins sitting in the shade, the only soul around. Is this Terry or is it Gary? I wonder.

I guess wrongly and say, "Hey, Gary," and Terry, accustomed to the confusion about his identity, corrects me. I'm embarrassed I didn't recognize him, since I've seen the twins around the plaza for years. Also, I photographed Gary a few years ago, beside a sign he put up to dissuade tourists from peering into his windows—a violation of privacy he and others here have experienced more than once.

I always intended to visit the twins in their mud-plastered adobe house on the plaza, reputed to be the oldest building in the area. It was the home of my great-great-great-grandfather Gervacio Ortega and his wife, Guadalupe Vigil. Gervacio, who was born in 1800 and died in the 1860s, was a cibolero, a hunter who annually made perilous forays out onto the Great Plains to pursue bison and trade with Indians. We know this from his two wills in the family documents. (He wrote the first 1851 as he lay in bed with an illness he thought would be fatal but proved not to be.) My grandma referred to the house affectionately as "*la casa de mi madre Vigila*—my mother Vigil's house," even though she never knew her great-grandma Guadalupe. On a folk map drawn by Sabino Trujillo (discussed in detail in my book *Sabino's Map*), Gervacio's house is marked "First House in the Plaza."

Sadly, the old house suffered a catastrophic fire just a few months ago, while Terry and Gary were asleep. They escaped with just the shirts on their backs, and only the walls of the house survived, their brittle adobe bricks baked to orange and black hues. Terry knows little of the history of the building; to him, it was a place to live, and one he was quite fond of. I relate to him a bit about Gervacio and bemoan the loss of such a historic structure. He laments the loss of his home.

On a whim, I decide to strain my memory to outline for him our family connections—practicing on my own, without any viejitos to straighten me out—since Gervacio is an ancestor we have in common.

"See, your grandfather Pedro Trujillo's father, Vidal Trujillo, was a son to Concepción, who lived in Río Chiquito and was married to my great-great-grandpa's sister, María Antonia Ortega—Gervacio's daughter. Vidal grew up in your house with his grandparents, Guadalupe and Gervacio. So Pedro and my great-grandfather were *primos hermanos*, first cousins—and that makes us cousins, too."

"No kidding?" Terry replies as we wander alongside crumbling buildings, adding dryly, "It just goes to show you can't pick your relatives."

As I say good-bye to Terry and drive on, I recall my mother's comment when we came across Terry here once: "That Gary or Terry or whichever he was—he sure looks like his dad, Nicky. Like they say, '*Del palo sale la estilla.*—From the stick comes the splinter.'"

We stop on the south side to visit Lorenzo Martínez, one of the last people living on the plaza who was born there. Lorenzo calls out his characteristic greeting: "*Órale*, Usner! How you been?" Although Lorenzo and I have no direct blood relationship I know of, he immediately reminds me of another tie between us, nearly as significant: "Hey, your grandma was my—how do they say? My, my . . ."

"Your madrina.—Your godmother," I fill in for him.

"Oh yeah, she was my madrina!" He grins. "She was a good woman—and a good friend to my mom."

This special relationship made Grandma and Lorenzo's mother Petronila comadres, and such nonblood kinship, compadrazgo, carried considerable weight in the old days. Compadres generally regarded each other with great affection. The *padrinos* were expected to take a special interest in and be involved with raising their godchild and, most importantly, to be available to assume care of a godchild who was orphaned. In the tight-knit network of extended family that was so important to the survival of these small communities, relatives tended to band together, because, as the dicho tells us, "*La sangre sin fuego hierve.*—Blood boils without fire." (Analagous to "Blood is thicker than water.") Compadrazgo was another type of glue that held the community together. I feel it now, between Lorenzo and me, two characters about as different as day and night.

I flash back to visits with Grandma to see Lorenzo's mother when I was a boy. Back then, Grandma always asked after her *ahijado* (godson) Lorencito, who was usually out terrorizing the plaza while we visited with his mother. Now I recall that young man as I gaze at the graying Lorenzo in front of me, as old as Petronila was in those long-ago visits—which doesn't seem such an advanced age now.

I haven't set foot in this house since I interviewed Petronila in 1989. The place feels empty with her gone. It seems odd to be visiting when she's not home. But Lorenzo welcomes me in and leans back on the couch. He offers me coffee, just like his mother used to do, but noticeably absent are the homemade bizcochitos I loved to devour.

Lorenzo points out portraits on the wall of his father, Biterbo Martínez, and his grandfather Antonio Martínez and other relatives in the plaza—alongside the ubiquitous religious prints that grace every Chimayó home. (Beneath Antonio's photograph a caption reads, "Antonio Martínez, Grandfather of Lorenzo Martínez who lives on the Plaza del Cerro.") After dozing for a few minutes, he leads me out to his tiny back patio, which opens onto spacious orchards that once belonged to the plaza patrón, Victor Ortega, my great-grandfather's brother. I'm swept away by the view of verdant fields sloping down to the thicketed Martínez Acequia, the dusty orange barrancas, and the blue mass of the Sangre de Cristo Mountains in the background. Lorencito lives in paradise, I decide.

He moseys over to another couch, this one outside, facing to the sweeping southern view, and slumps down to take it all in.

DICHOS ABOUT FATE AND HARDSHIP

Aquí me metí en camisa de once varas.
    I got myself into a shirt eleven varas long. (I got myself into trouble I don't know how to get out of.)

De la suerte y de la muerte no hay quien se escape.
    From fate and from death, no one can escape. (Luck or the lack of is just as inevitable as death.)

De más alto se han visto caer.
    From higher up they have been seen to fall. (Said of people bragging about their high status.)

Día de mucho, vísperas de nada.
    Day of plenty, evening of nothing. (Fortune is unpredictable; after a time of plenty, scarcity may well follow.)

Él que de suerte es, de dondequiera le llueve.
    For one who is lucky, it rains on him everywhere he goes. (A lucky person finds good fortune everywhere he turns.)

Él que nace pa' tamales, del cielo le caen las hojas.
    For one who is born to make tamales, corn-husk leaves fall from heaven. (Said of a lucky person.)

Él que nace pa' trabajos, desde la cuna los pasa.
    One who is born for misfortune starts having it from the cradle. (Some people are born for trouble.)

Él que nace para guajes hasta jumates no para.
   One who is born to gourds won't stop until he becomes a dipper. (Someone born to be great won't stop until he reaches the top.)

Escapó la gallina más que sea sin pluma.
   The chicken escaped, even though it lost its feathers. (Said of one who recovers from a serious illness, an accident, or a close brush with death.)

Mal ajeno del pelo cuelga.
   Another's misfortune hangs from a hair. (Said when one cares little for someone else's misfortune.)

Natural y figura hasta la sepultura.
   Disposition and character will follow one to the grave.

No falta un roto pa' un descosido ni un sordo pa' un aturdido.
   There is always a torn one for a ripped one and a deaf one for a stunned one. (There is always somebody you can match up with.)

No hay mal que por bien no venga.
   There is no evil that doesn't bring good. (Dark clouds have silver linings.)

No hay mejor experiencia como la que el tiempo da.
   There is no better experience than that which time gives you.

No por mucho madrugar amanece más temprano.
   The dawn won't come sooner because you get up early.

Poco daño espanta y mucho amansa.
   One mishap scares you, and many tame you. (The more hardships you suffer, the more patience you learn.)

Si una puerta se cierra, quinientas se abren.
   If one door closes, five hundred open.

Somos como los cubos de noria, unos suben y otros bajan.
    We are like buckets in a well—some go up and others, down.

Te toca si te sientas en el tocador.
    It will happen to you if you make it happen. (It's your turn if you take it.)

Ya está el cuero en el agua.
    The hide is already in the water. (It's too late to do anything about a mistake.)

Ya la espiga va pa' abajo.
    The spike of wheat is already bending. (Said when a person is getting old.)

Ya le anda la lumbre a los aparejos.
    The fire is already up to his pack saddles. (Trouble is about to catch up with him.)

Benerito Vigil at the transfer station, ca. 1995.

Benerito on La Otra Banda

Dios resiste a los soberbios y da gracia a los humildes.
God denies the wise and gives grace to the humble.

On this visit to Chimayó, Mom and I decide to visit a neighborhood that the people from the Plaza del Cerro refer to simply as *la otra banda* (the other bank), since it's on the other, south side of the Santa Cruz River. This little neighborhood is situated near Potrero and across the river from Los Ranchos. It also goes by the toponym Los Vigiles, since it is populated mostly by the extended Vigil family.

Benerito Vigil and I became friends years ago when he managed the county refuse transfer station on the road to Nambé. Everyone knew Benerito, and he knew everyone—and their trash. He and I became friends after many days of conversation there as flies buzzed around and pickup trucks full of rubbish came full and left empty—usually after their drivers had had a good conversation with Benerito.

One can't help but like Benerito, with his rugged yet cherubic face and the twinkle in his eye. Besides being gregarious and a great conversationalist, he is a master of Spanglish profanity. I've learned a lot of special words from him, picking up where I left off when running around Chimayó as a child. He always greets me with a cheerful "*¡Cabrón!*" when I visit him in his family compound on la otra banda. Today is no exception. He doesn't at first see my mother in the car and comes out of his house affectionately shouting the usual epithet, followed by a string of a few others for good measure.

"What the f—— you doing here?" he asks—and then he realizes who is seated next to me on the passenger side. "*¡Discúlpeme, señora!*" he pleads, asking her forgiveness and offering a more palatable greeting.

Benerito is delighted to see my mother, and once she's over her shock and embarrassment, my mother warms to him, too. He immediately sets about asking for her family. Mom does the same. Benerito is a couple of decades younger than she is, but they nonetheless share many memories of old times. He warmly remembers my grandmother and her four sisters—Juanita, Petrita, Melita, and Candelaria—as well as my mother's younger brother, Bobby. He and Mom compare recollections of their time at the John Hyson Elementary School, which they both attended, years apart. And of course they go through a genealogical labyrinth, only to conclude they can't pinpoint a connection in kin, although my mother and I are quick to point out we have a strong Vigil line in our ancestry, including Guadalupe Vigil ("mi madre Vigila"), who was married to my great-great-great-grandfather, Gervacio Ortega. Then of course my great-great-aunt, Gelacia Chávez, married Longino Vigil from Cundiyó. And in our papers, a Juan Antonio Begil shows up on a land sale dated 1786. Both of our families refer to the Vigils from Cundiyó as primos, so we agree that surely there is a connection between us somewhere in the multitude of marriages and births stretching between 1786 and now.

As soon as Benerito turns his head away from the car window, he seems to forget Mom is with me, and he lapses back into his coarse profanity. The subject of the local bully comes up, with reference to how he used to harass Benerito at the transfer station. In fact, he has harassed just about everyone in Chimayó, including me, and talking about him prompts Benerito to spit on the ground and emit a string of eloquent bilingual expletives. I take notes on the terminology and inflection of his invective as my mother winces.

I leave Mom in the car while I walk over to the abandoned house next to Benerito's, a simple adobe, built in the old L-shaped, pitched-roof style and now crumpling into ruin. Behind the house loom rugged, steep barrancas, bright orange red in color, bordered at their base by blazing yellow cottonwoods that line the Acequia del Potrero. A kind of fallout zone of discarded machinery and household items surrounds the house. Its rusted roof lifts into the sunshine. We're on the edge here—of Chimayó and of the cultivated land, which is watered by a winding finger of the Potrero acequia. Above the ditch and houses, the arid lands parch in the sun, in a vast landscape empty of human habitation. But it hasn't always been that way. I've walked out there enough to know of

Abandoned car in la otra banda, *2010.*

extensive Pueblo ruins, inhabited some six hundred years ago by hundreds of people who depended on this "vacant" land nearly as much as on the bottomlands by the river. Out there too are old trails where Chimayosos led their livestock, where *curanderos* gathered herbs. But nowadays, very few venture out beyond the roads in the settled land by the waterways.

Benerito has given me free rein to go inside the house, although he can't understand why I would want to. "There's nothing but death there," he says. "We never go in." Walking down to the house, I remember on an earlier visit Benerito told me his Tío Alfredo died in bed when the house burned in a fire ignited by his burning cigarette.

I step through the doorway and see scorched bedsprings lying on the floor.

The walls and ceilings still bear the marks of smoke and flames. I'm fascinated by the ruins, especially the odd details: a coatrack made of two battered boards painted pastel green and yellow; pink paint and raw mud on a crumbling wall; muddy trails left on paint and plaster by rivulets of rain; gaping holes in the wooden floor beside the dust-filled porcelain bathtub; smoke-stained window glass refracting images of abandoned vehicles shimmering in the sun outside.

I exit the house through a doorway beside an apricot tree that leans, spilling a rich carpet of golden leaves. Tiptoeing around a caved-in septic tank that gapes like a pit trap, I walk over to peer into the old stone-and-mud *soterrano* (cellar) out back. Its roof has almost completely collapsed, but I'm able to squeeze inside with just enough room to maneuver to a window and look out through it, back toward the house.

Evening approaches. The light has grown gloomy. Mom waits in the car, chatting with Benerito, now in polite Spanish. From somewhere in the cottonwoods along the acequia, a great horned owl begins to hoot, and I'm reminded of a story about *brujería* (witchcraft) that Grandma told me. It was about a woman from Rincón who was alleged to be a bruja. Like all brujas, she turned into an owl at night and flew about doing evil deeds. The setting for the story as Grandma painted it looked very much like the scene before me: an abandoned house with a haunting history; a peaked, rusted roof; trees rustling in the gathering darkness; an owl hooting; and, yes, a sliver of moon hanging in the sky.

Listening to the hooting, I recall a little song about an owl Grandma used to sing to entertain me:

"¡Tecolotito valiente!	"Brave little owl!
¡Tecolotito valiente!	Brave little owl!
¿Qué haces en esa sotea?	What are you doing on that roof?
¿Qué haces en esa sotea?"	What are you doing on that roof?"
"Mirando los borracheros,	"Looking at the drunkards,
Mirando los borracheros,	Looking at the drunkards,
Empinarse la botella,	Tipping the bottle,
Empinarse la botella."	Tipping the bottle."
Pobrecito animalito,	Poor little animal,
Tiene hambre tecolotito,	He's hungry, that little owl,
Ooooo, oooo . . .	Ooooo, oooo . . .

Alfredo Vigil's abandoned house, la otra banda, 2009.

DICHOS ABOUT CHARACTER

Al que va a la bodega por vez se le cuenta, beba o no beba.
　　People will talk when someone goes into a bar, whether he drinks or not.

Anda buscando pies al gato.
　　She's looking for feet on the cat. (She is suspiciously looking for something.)

Anda dándose golpes de pecho.
　　He is going around beating his breast. (Said of someone who is a braggart or someone feeling sorry for himself.)

Anda haciendo tripas corazones.
　　She is making guts into hearts. (She is trying her best to be brave after a tragedy; putting a good face on a bad situation.)

Anda tirando manotadas de 'hogado.
　　He's flailing like a drowning man. (He's got himself into trouble and doesn't know how to get out.)

Aquí en la gloria y en el infierno ardiendo.
　　Here in heaven, and in hell burning. (A person will pay later for all the good times she is having.)

Allí no engordan perros flacos.
　　Skinny dogs don't get fat there. (Said about families who are stingy.)

Caballo ajeno, espuelas propias: el mundo es mío.
>Borrowed horse, my own spurs: the world is mine. (Said of someone who is having a good time with things that don't belong to him.)

Cada chango en su columpio.
>Each monkey on his swing. (Everybody does his own thing.)

Cada maestrito tiene su librito.
>Each little teacher has his own little book. (Each person has his own way of doing things.)

Grabielita Ortega in Ranchitos, 2011.

Grabielita in Ranchitos

Si no es santo es porque no la cuelgan.
If she is not a saint, it's only because they don't hang her on the wall.

After we check on Grandma's house, Mom and I decide to stop in on Grabielita Ortega. Neither of us has spoken to her in perhaps a decade. She and Grandma were dear friends, as well as relatives through marriage. When I was growing up, we visited Grabielita and her son Roger, a wonderful soul born into a body with multiple disabilities. Grabielita cared for him for all of his fifty-four years. He never left his bed, and she never left him. Because of this and because of her perpetually upbeat and selfless manner, Grandma considered Grabielita a saint, and I know of no one in Chimayó who would disagree.

Grabielita lives less than a mile from the Plaza del Cerro in the Ranchitos neighborhood, on land that belonged to her father-in-law, Rumaldo Ortega. Mom says he claimed the land through the federal government's *pequeñas tenencias* program, the Homestead Act. Ranchitos is located along an arroyo that carries water only during summer storms. The fields and fine orchards here get their water from the Acequia de la Cañada Ancha, which flows from the tiny Río Quemado just upstream in Río Chiquito. It took some clever homegrown engineering and hard labor to divert the Quemado through the hills and into the Cañada Ancha arroyo, but a large part of Chimayó owes its existence to the ditch.

Rumaldo was an older brother to my great-grandpa, Reyes Ortega, so he was my grandmother's uncle. They say Rumaldo married Rosarito Rodríguez when she was only twelve or thirteen years old and he was twenty-three. Rumaldo and Rosarito's son Anastacio married Grabielita and had a long and fruitful marriage, although Grabielita has been a widow now for forty-five years.

Grabielita breaks into a giant smile and hugs us warmly as only primos will. Her greeting to us, called out in an emotion-laden Spanish with an inflection and idiom all her own—"*¡Buenas tardes! ¡Mire quién viene!*—Good afternoon! Look who's coming!"—brings me back instantly to those times when Grandma and I used to walk over to see her. At ninety-eight, she is one of those few remaining in Chimayó who seldom use English and, if they do, modulate it with such an accent that it sounds like a foreign tongue.

Grabielita's sister Eremita just died a week ago, at the age of 106, Grabielita tells us, and then she enumerates the rest of her seven siblings and their statuses. All five of her brothers are dead, but two sisters remain alive.

"*¿Sabes cuántos nietos tengo?*—Do you know how many grandchildren I have?" she asks me. And then she answers her own question, "*Nietos tenía diez y ocho, pero dos muertos.*—I had eighteen, but two are dead." Then she turns to my mother, "*¿Te acuerdas de la Joanna, la que mataron? Y nunca supieron quién la mató.*—Do you remember Joanna, the one they killed? And no one ever found out who did it."

"*Pero tengo vivos* sixteen.—But sixteen are still alive. Y *tengo* great-grandchildren, thirty," Grabielita goes on. "*Y luego tengo quince* great-great-grandchildren.—And I have fifteen great-great-grandchildren," she continues, mixing it up with Spanish and English as she names them all. She breaks out laughing.

"*¡Ya eres nanarabuela!*—You're already a great-great-grandma!" Mom exclaims.

"*¡O, linda!*—Oh, darling!" Grabielita squeals and chuckles.

"*Yo tengo quince nietos y ocho bisnietos.*—I have fifteen grandchildren and eight great-grandchildren," Mom adds.

"*¿Ocho no más?*—Only eight?" Grabielita comments. "*No es mucho.*—That's not much."

"*Yo tengo una hija.*—I have one daughter," I pitch in.

Startled, Grabielita asks, "*¿Una no más?*—Just one? *¿Y nietos, nada?*—And no grandkids?"

A bit taken aback at my lack of reproductive prowess, she asks Mom about her children. Mom names her five kids and, when Grabielita asks, tells her where each lives.

"*¿Una hija en Cundiyó?*—You have a daughter in Cundiyó?" Grabielita asks. "*¿Con quién se casó allí?*—Whom did she marry there?" she queries, curious because she herself comes from Cundiyó.

"*O, se casó con un gringo.*—Oh, she married a gringo," my mother says. "*No es Cundiyoso.*—Not a Cundiyoso."

"*¿Cuándo venites la última vez?*—When were you last here?" Grabielita asks my mother.

"*La Elena y yo venimos yo no sé cúando.*—Helen and I came some time back."

"*La Elena, ¿cómo está? ¿Ya es viejita también?*—And Helen, how is she? Is she an old lady now, too?" Grabielita asks, giggling.

"*Es poca viejita.*—She's kind of old," Mom chuckles. "*Somos de la misma edad.*—She and I are the same age."

"*¿La misma edad? ¡Qué lindo!*—The same age? Oh, how wonderful," Grabielita exclaims with another giggle.

"*Toda mi familia vive aquí cerca.*—All my family lives nearby," Grabielita goes on, proudly. "*Nomás los bebés, Tom y Harold, viven lejos, en Albuquerque.*—Only the babies, Tom and Harold, live far away, in Albuquerque," she adds, speaking of her sons, who are in their sixties.

Grabielita describes her children and grandchildren living around her. They're on all sides, and they come to see her daily.

"*Y luego tenía a mi Miguelito.*—And then I had my Miguelito. *Vivía aquí cerca, en su traila, hijo de la Clara y el Arturo.*—He lived right here in the trailer. He was Arturo and Clara's son. *Pero se murió de una enfermedad.*—But he died of an illness."

Grabielita's granddaughter, Peggy Sue, comes in and hugs my mother.

"Look how beautiful you are!" she exclaims.

"*Venían a visitarme.*—They came to visit me," Grabielita informs her, nodding toward us proudly.

"*¡Qué bonito, Grandma!*—How wonderful, Grandma," Peggy Sue replies, holding Grabielita's face in her hands and beaming a mile-wide smile. Then she embraces me warmly, even though she and I have never met. She jumps into the conversation and elaborates on the story of the recent death of Miguel, her brother.

"He had been very sick and living away, but then he came home and moved in right here, next door to Grandma. He held a very special place in her heart. He was her first grandchild.

"And he was waiting to see little Grandma. I felt it. One of his uncles took her to see him. And within two hours of seeing her—he got her hand and she prayed with him. And he said, 'Jesus loves me,' and he closed his eyes and passed away. He had a very beautiful death. But he had to wait for Grandma. *¿Qué no, Grandma?*—Right, Grandma?"

Grabielita shrugs and says, "*Sí . . . ay, linda. Así es la vida.*—Yes . . . oh, dear. Life is that way."

DICHOS ABOUT CHARACTER

Cada uno en su corazón juzga al ajeno.
    Each in his heart judges others. (You judge others by what you are yourself.)

Candil de la calle, oscuridad de su casa.
    Lighted candle on the street, darkness at the home. (Said of one who is friendly and outgoing with with strangers, but cruel at home.)

Caras vemos, corazones no sabemos.
    We see faces, but we don't know hearts. (The face doesn't reveal the heart's feelings.)

Como canta el abad, responde el sacristán.
    Whatever the priest recites, the altar boy answers. (Said of one who doesn't think for himself but does everything another commands without question.)

Con el colador que medimos vamos ser medidos.
    With the strainer that we use to measure, we shall be measured.

Con la vara que mides serás medido.
    With the yardstick that you measure others, you shall be measured.

Cuando no le llueve, le gotea.
    When it doesn't rain on him, it drips on him. (Said of a lucky person.)

Cuida tu casa y deja la ajena.
    Mind your own house and leave others' alone.

De cuero ajeno, largas correas.
>From someone else's hide, long straps. (It's easy to be generous with somebody else's property.)

De los dos no se hace uno.
>From the two of them you can't make one. (Even together, the two of them are worth nothing.)

Del palo sale la astilla.
>From the stick comes the splinter. (Like parent, like child.)

Dos agujas no se pican.
>Two needles can't prick each other. (Said of two people of the same bad temperament.)

El bien y el mal a la cara salen.
>Good and evil are reflected in the face.

El diablo no duerme.
>The devil doesn't sleep.

Esequiel Trujillo, Los Ojuelos, 2009.

Esequiel in Los Ojuelos

Con la vara que mides, serás medido.
With the yardstick that you measure others, you shall be measured.

I'm on a quest to find Esequiel Trujillo, whom I barely know but greatly admire. Esequiel has described to me how to find his home, and when I lived in Chimayó I often watched him drive past my house in his old truck on his way to the cluster of buildings among which his house stood. The older generations call this little neighborhood Los Ojuelos, a reference to the nearby Arroyo de los Ojuelos, or Arroyo of the Little Springs. Some say the neighborhood is called Los Abuelos, which means "the grandfathers" and could refer to the Abuelos, characters prominent in the Matachines dance. I don't think so, but it's a moot point in any case; almost no one uses the old name of this neighborhood anymore.

With some trepidation I drive down Esequiel's way on this warm autumn afternoon, skirting the dramatic barrancas at the northern edge of the Santa Cruz Valley. The looming presence of the barrancas makes this one of the most picturesque parts of Chimayó. The striking contrast between the dry formations and the verdant cottonwoods and fields below demonstrates the dramatic effect of irrigation water from the humble Acequia de la Cañada Ancha, a small ditch that nevertheless is the longest ditch in Chimayó. It's also a very old ditch. A record in our papers from 1817 mentions it, and it was certainly around much earlier. Way up in Río Chiquito a small *presa* diverts the water for this ditch from the Río Quemado. Culverts called *canoas*, which back in the day were made from hollowed-out logs, channel the water through a break in the sandy hills and carry it out of the Quemado drainage and over into the

Cañada Ancha. There it begins its long, winding route along the northern edge of Chimayó, irrigating some of the sandiest soils in the valley and nurturing a string of hardy cottonwood trees. One conduit crossing an arroyo is held up by a line of wrecked car chassis, jammed vertically into the sand.

I make a turn down an eroded dirt driveway at the base of a gigantic sandstone spire, just past a dilapidated old barn and corrals. I toot the horn outside the first house I come to. A sixty-something man in a white muscle shirt comes out to greet me. He walks with a slight limp as he ambles over to my truck and offers a handshake. I expect suspicion but instead am met with openhearted friendliness. He introduces himself as Leroy Trujillo, a cousin to Esequiel. We chat about his relationship with his primo Esequiel and other Trujillos in Chimayó. He tells me of his difficult battle with Parkinson's disease, which he says is slowly overtaking him. He points down the driveway and tells me where to find Esequiel's house: down by the old Chevy flatbed.

I creep slowly past a few relatively new houses, a 1955 Chevy Impala sedan stranded in a forest of weeds and trees, and a rundown adobe with once-elegant Territorial-style trim around the windows and doors. I cross a lateral ditch that flows from the Cañada Ancha to Esequiel's property.

I turn off the driveway at the Chevy truck, a 1946 model, its blue paint weathered and rusted, the red wooden railing of its bed now cracked and chipped and bowed outward. The truck hasn't moved in years; it's hemmed in by stacks of adobe bricks, scrap lumber, and other assorted odds and ends. A scattering of newer abandoned cars and trucks are parked at a respectful distance from the senior truck. A furious black Rottweiler, chained to the front of the truck like its personal guardian, dissuades me from examining the vehicle more closely.

The farm gate to Esequiel's driveway stands open. I park outside and walk through. To my right a weathered old outbuilding stands beside yet another abandoned car, a 1960s-era Oldsmobile, on its hood a Boone's Farm wine box filled with used car parts. I keep a cautious eye toward the Rottweiler behind me, watching his chain and collar strain close to the breaking point as he leaps and snarls—and then I'm blindsided by a black pit bull racing toward me from the porch of the house. I hold my ground and snap a gruff command: "*¡Vete!*— Go on!" She cowers and circles away toward a cardboard box filled with whimpering puppies. Esequiel emerges from his doorway, shushing the dog into further submission, then turns to me with a bemused smile.

"*¡Mire no más! ¡Buenas tardes le dé Dios!*—Will you look at that! May God grant you a good afternoon!" Esequiel exclaims. Then, pointing to the dog, he says, "*Perro que ladra no muerde.*—A dog that barks doesn't bite."

I call out in the same formal greeting of old—"*Buenas tardes le dé Dios*"—and remind him of our visit at Magdalena's a while back. I go on to introduce myself anyway, in the way of all tribal people: "*Soy Don Usner, nieto de la Benigna Chávez, de allá, de la Plaza del Cerro.*—I'm Don Usner, Benigna Chávez's grandson, from up there in the Plaza del Cerro."

"*Sí, me acuerdo bien.*"—Yes, I remember well," he responds. He asks for my mother and the rest of my family, and we reminisce about that fine day when we all visited at Magdalena's house.

Glancing around his place, I ask about the old truck. He bought it nearly new and used it for many years. It's only recently been parked there, he says, and he plans to repair it. We walk over to inspect it, the Rottweiler cowering away at Esequiel's command. I peer into the cab, through thick, cracked windows. The windshield bears an incongruous, outdated sticker for LAMPF, or the Los Alamos Meson Physics Facility, a powerful linear accelerator located at Los Alamos National Laboratory. (Esequiel once worked there.) Inside the truck I see several cottonwood rounds piled on the front seat. These are the beginnings of drums, he explains, which he makes and uses in the Matachines dances. "*Yo tengo uno muy grande que me dio mi hijo, en la casa.*—I have a really big drum my son gave me, in the house," he tells me. "*Yo te enseño.*—I'll show you."

Looking up the driveway, I point out the old house I admired on the way down. Esequiel tells me he was born there and that the house belonged to his father, Don Benigno Trujillo, the renowned sobador who used to work on my grandmother's knee. Esequiel is particularly delighted when I tell him, again, how much Grandma relied on Don Benigno and praised his great skill.

"*Decía mi grandma que don Benigno era el único que le ayudaba con su rodilla lastimada. No quería nada a los doctores.*—She used to say Don Benigno was the only one who could help her injured knee. She didn't like doctors at all," I explain.

I don't yet mention the story Grandma used to tell about Don Benigno, who was the darling of all the old women in Chimayó, with their universally bad knees. The *chiste* (joke) was that, while he was massaging them, Don Benigno would say to the viejitas, "*La lastimada queda poco más arribita.*"—The injury is just a little higher up," and he earnestly endeavored to work his way up past their knobby knees. The women would reel him in and preserve their honor, but they didn't seem to consider his affections lecherous and always asked him back.

"*O sí, sabía mucho.*—Oh yes, he knew a lot," Esequiel agrees. He points to the house next door and says, "*Allí vivía él.*—He lived there."

Esequiel and I walk over to Don Benigno's house and launch into a discussion of my relationship to his Trujillo clan. Eventually we climb the family tree enough to find that his grandfather, Guadalupe Trujillo, from the large Trujillo family of Rincón de los Trujillos, was brother to Severiano Trujillo, who married my great-grandfather's sister, Senaida Ortega. Thus we are connected, but only through marriage.

The Trujillo name goes way back in our family papers. The first mention comes in 1792, on a land sale from Antonio Trujillo, a resident of Abiquiú, to Salvador Medina, somewhere in Santa Cruz. Any possible link through that line, or our link through marriage several generations ago, seems tenuous and distant, but it's good enough. "*Es que por eso les decíamos primos a los Ortegas.*—That's why we called the Ortegas our cousins," Esequiel proclaims, in reference to my grandmother's family. Our footing as primos is secure.

"*Siempre está bienvenido aquí. Tome todos los retratos que quiere.*—You're always welcome here. Take all the pictures you want," he assures me. "*Pase para adentro.*—Come on in." And he puts on water for coffee.

DICHOS ABOUT CHARACTER

El maestro Ciruela, que no sabía leer y puso escuela.
   Mr. Plum, who didn't know how to read, started a school. (Said of someone who doesn't know anything and yet wants to tell others how to do things.)

El más ciego es él que no quiere ver.
   The blindest one is he who doesn't want to see.

Él que al pobre cierra la puerta, la del cielo no halla abierta.
   One who closes the door on the poor will not find the gates of heaven open.

Él que boca tiene, a Roma va.
   One who has a mouth goes to Rome. (One who speaks up will go far.)

Él que come y canta, loco se levanta.
   One who eats and sings gets up acting crazy.

Él que con lobos anda a aullar se enseña.
   One who goes around with wolves learns how to howl.

Él que con perros se acuesta con garrapatas se levanta.
   One who goes to sleep with dogs wakes up with fleas. (Bad companions will lead you astray.)

Él que con sabios anda algo se le prende.
   One who goes around with wise men will learn something.

Él que da y quita, le sale una corcovita.
    One who gives a gift and then takes it away gets a hump on his back.

Él que de cuarenta no está rico se queda pa' borrico.
    One who is not rich by forty will have the life of a burro. (If you don't make it by forty you will always be poor.)

Él que del costo huye, huye del provecho.
    One who runs away from the expense runs away from the benefits.

Él que en hambre vive en el hambre muere.
    One who lives in hunger dies in hunger. (One who lives a miserly life dies miserable.)

Juan Trujillo and his Chihuahua in Potrero, 2009.

Juan Trujillo and the Capilla de San Antonio del Potrero

No es el león como lo pintan.
The lion is not the way they paint him to be.

I drop into Chimayó and turn off in Potrero, the first plaza of Chimayó encountered when coming from Santa Fe. Here stands the celebrated Santuario de Chimayó, an adobe church built by my great-great-great-great-great-grandfather Bernardo Abeyta.

On occasion I came to Mass here as a child, always impressed by the interior artwork, with a sense of awe bordering on foreboding. These renderings of religious figures conveyed to me a mysterious vision of spirituality, their facial expressions contrasting dark fatalism with ineffable grace. Father Roca's droning sermons in impenetrable, Catalan-inflected Spanish only added to my feelings of wonderment.

We have close ties to this church. As my mother tells it, our ancestor, Manuel Chávez, came with his father, Rafael Chávez, on a visit to the santuario in about 1815. They were from the community of Los Chávez, close to Bernalillo. (The Chávez family was among the sheep patrones of the Río Abajo in New Mexico, landowners who possessed large estates and generated great wealth in the sheep trade.) Rafael returned to Los Chávez, but Manuel stayed in Chimayó and married Bernardo's daughter María del Carmen. He was twenty-three years old; she was fifteen. "This started the Chávez clan in Potrero," my mother explained to me. "Before then there were no Chávezes in Chimayó."

Rafael Chávez was a leader of Los Hermanos (the Penitentes) in Los Chávez, near Bernalillo. He had come to Chimayó to visit Don Bernardo Abeyta, who was an *hermano mayor* (elder brother) in the organization and may have been one of the founders of the Hermanos brotherhood when it blossomed in northern New Mexico. Along with the Chávez family name, Manuel brought with him his sheep, which he pastured in the *potreros* (pastures) of Potrero.

The plaza of Potrero appears for the first time in our documents on a note appended to an 1829 paper authorizing a sale of land near the Plaza del Cerro from Pascual and Nicolás Ortega to their brother, Manuel Pablo. We have many more recent family connections to Potrero. My great-grandfather, Juan Clímaco Chávez, came from Potrero, and my great-grandfather Reyes Ortega's sister married Juan Clímaco's grandfather, Manuel Chávez. (This meant my grandmother married her father's grandnephew, or her first cousin once removed.)

When I was growing up we would load up the car with flowers, real and plastic, as well as hoes and shovels, to visit the *campo santo* (cemetery) in Potrero each year on Memorial Day. Until the early 1900s, local people (or at least some prominent citizens) were buried inside the santuario; my great-great-grandpa José Ramón Ortega, his mother, María Petrita Ortega, and many other antepasados were laid to rest beneath the hallowed ground of the church, alongside the church's founder, Bernardo Abeyta. (Because of the practice, by the eighteenth century many churches in New Mexico were overflowing with bodies, sometimes stacked five or six deep beneath the floor.) Longtime efforts to stop church burials finally took effect, though, and all the dead were taken to the "new" cemetery just down the road.

It always seemed to be sunny and hot in late May as we wound our way amid the gravestones to find the markers for our dearly departed. We worked hard to clear the weeds and cactus, mangle the Siberian elms (which always came back with a vengeance), dust off the stones, and decorate them with our humble floral arrangements. Each year I remembered better how to find the family graves among the hodgepodge of stone, wooden, and paper markers. I was proud when I finally could locate all the graves of relatives, although there were only three we tended regularly. The oldest was bordered by a small iron fence and marked with a simple stone commemorating the short life of my great-grandmother Genoveva Archuleta Quintana, who died in childbirth in 1919 at the age of forty-one. Her section of the graveyard was nearly overgrown with weeds. In the newer part we cleared debris from my grandfather

Abedón Chávez's sloping slab of concrete, set in 1949, and from the newer (1968) grave of Mom's brother, Leo Chávez.

Campo santo visits were by no means entirely somber affairs. They often turned into cheerful social gatherings. We ran into people we hadn't seen for a long time, met relatives we had never known, and expressed condolences to friends and family at fresh mounds. It made the sweaty work interesting.

After the cleanup at the Catholic campo santo, we would travel across the valley to the Plaza del Cerro to tend to the graves of family members who were buried in the newer, Presbyterian cemetery. This burial ground occupies a hillside on land my great-grandfather Reyes Ortega sold for a nominal sum to the Presbyterian Church. Reyes had drifted from the Catholic Church when he elected to send his daughters to the new Presbyterian mission school, thinking they could get a better education there than that offered in the public school. His split from Catholicism also resulted from the reprimand he endured from a priest on the pulpit, who criticized Reyes for performing marriages of couples outside the Catholic Church. In doing this, Reyes was merely fulfilling his duties as a duly elected justice of the peace, but the activity did not put him in good stead with church authorities—and the public rebuke stung him greatly.

Reyes was not buried near his wife and many other kin in the ancestral cemetery in Potrero. Instead, his headstone stands on a hill overlooking the Plaza del Cerro, surrounded by the graves of three of his daughters, Petrita, Juanita, and Melita, and of his son-in-law Isaías Ortega. They lie in rest beside several dozen others who joined the *herejes* (heretics), as the Protestants were sometimes called, who came to the valley in 1900. The arrival of the *protestantes* encumbered Reyes's descendants with a cross-valley journey of remembrance each spring, as they went from one cemetery to another.

Since those old days, the original campo santo in Potrero has filled up. Deceased Catholics are carted to a still newer Catholic cemetery, isolated from the irrigated valley and surrounded by dramatic barrancas. There we interred Grandma as well as two nieces who died just after birth and a nephew who died tragically young. Our Memorial Day rounds have now expanded to reach this, the third burying ground we must visit.

I'm not stopping at any of those cemeteries today, though. I'm on my way to visit a small chapel that graces a hilltop above Potrero, the Capilla de San Antonio.

Capilla de San Antonio, Potrero, 2009.

The whitewashed San Antonio chapel takes in a spectacular view of the Chimayó Valley. The very site elevates the spirit. In Santa Fe and other places, the wealthy clamor for the right to build on hilltops with prime vistas. Here, for the most part, the prime-view real estate is occupied by shrines, part of a habit of molding the human community to the land. Small clusters of buildings and mobile homes wrap around the hill and its rocky neighbors, following the natural watercourses and acequias. From the vantage of the hilltop at the San Antonio chapel, everything made by people appears clearly subordinate to the landscape. People have fit into the place.

The Pueblos also maintained shrines on high points like these. One of the papers we have mentions a place "*donde resavan los originales*—where the originals used to pray" as a land boundary. "Originals" may refer to the early Spanish colonists, but it could also refer to Native people. In any case, perhaps this hill, with its bird's-eye perspective on human endeavors, has been reserved as a place to pray since precolonial times.

I walk up the hill to the capilla, following a well-worn path. A stick holds closed the hasp on the small double doors. This place needs no earthly protection—at least not yet. The concrete slab outside the door bears the inscription "5–22–56, JMS," recording the date of completion of the chapel by Juan M. Sandoval, its builder, whose grandson maintains the structure and lives nearby. Inside the tiny room, a cluster of statues of saints and other holy figures crowds a small altar festooned with a vase of plastic flowers. A statue of San Antonio takes center stage as the tallest figure in the group, flanked by three or four smaller, nearly identical versions. A bas-relief of the Virgin with child hangs above them all, shadowed by peeled paint dangling from the ceiling. A small textile depicting the Virgin of Guadalupe glows, backlit, in one window, while a crucifix made of barbed wire is silhouetted in another. In a spiral-bound notebook visitors have entered their names and comments and pleas for the intercession of San Antonio.

As a mediator for humankind, San Antonio specializes in helping people find misplaced items, missing persons, and anything else lost, including jobs or lovers. He is one of the most popular saints in Chimayó. There have been many occasions when people in my family have called upon San Antonio, the most dramatic being the time when Grandma's cousin, Ramón Quintana, went missing. It seems that the three-year-old Ramón disappeared while the family was picking piñón in the Sierra de Pecos, as they then called the Sangre de Cristo Mountains and their foothills. San Antonio answered the family's long prayers when Ramón showed up at the santuario, shoes in hand, days after he disappeared. Somehow he managed to travel on foot down from the mountains to the holy shrine. He barely had learned to talk, but he described the guide who led him as a woman dressed in blue. Apparently, San Antonio sent the Virgin Mary to do the legwork.

Although I don't count myself among the true believers in this kind of divine intervention, I have, in desperation, put in a request or two with San Antonio. To my surprise, it seems to work—especially if I have Grandma, my mother, or some other relative with a little more clout than me submit a prayer to him. Grandma was always willing to do this, but she was careful to add the proviso, "*Si Dios no quiere, santos no pueden.*—If God does not will it, saints can't do it."

Of course, this kind of on-demand supplication to San Antonio is strongly discouraged by the faithful as a cheap shortcut. I'm reminded of the dicho about people like me, who call upon divine help only when all else fails: "*No se acuerdan de Santa Bárbara hasta que hacen los truenos.*—They don't remember to pray to Santa Bárbara until they find themselves in trouble." Or another one: "*Esperando el bien de Dios sin saber por dónde viene.*—Waiting for the grace of God without knowing where it will come from."

On a lighter note, I learned from Grandma a little rhyme mimicking a prayer from a single woman to San Antonio, asking for help in finding a husband. Grandma used to tell it like this: "There was this woman who wanted to get married real badly, so she called on San Antonio, who is supposed to find things for you. She prayed to him:

'*San Antonito, San Antonaso*	'Little Saint Anthony, big old Saint Anthony
¿Cuándo me caso?'	When will I marry?'

"San Antonio granted the woman's wish, but the husband turned out to be no good, so she prayed to San Antonio again:

'*San Antonito, piesitos, manitas,*	'San Antonito, with your little feet and hands,
¿Cuándo me lo quitas?'	When will you get rid of him?'

"The moral of the story," Grandma would say with a wink, "is to watch what you ask for, especially from San Antonio!"

Outside the capilla, I climb higher up the hill to look down on the building against a backdrop of the Chimayó Valley in fall color. Turning around, I notice there is a house higher up on the hill, behind me, and I recall that it belongs to my friend Julian Sandoval, Juan Sandoval's grandson. So much for my theory about hilltops being reserved for places of worship. Now that technology allows it, high points are fair game for building any kind of structure. I realize there probably would have been homes on the hilltops long ago if people had access to heavy machinery for making roads and to drilling equipment for digging deep wells. People confined themselves to the valleys because they had to. Glancing across the valley, I see several low hills that have been leveled to accommodate double-wide trailers.

The window on the east side of the chapel reflects golden cottonwoods below in a nearly perfect mirror image. I take some photographs of this remarkable phenomenon, then amble back down the pathway to the road, where I encounter Juan Trujillo, cutting weeds by his house. I knew Juan when I lived in Chimayó, and we're on friendly terms.

"*¡Cabrón!*" he greets me, in the same manner as Benerito, his neighbor a half-mile down the ditch. "What you doing around here?"

Cabrón (bastard) is one of those malleable words that is fundamentally a profanity but can be used in an inoffensive, even endearing way. It may seem a crude greeting, but coming from Juan in this context, it conveys no malice.

Grandma used to say that people from Potrero spoke "with rough language." By way of illustration, she told the story about a woman from the Plaza del Cerro, where Grandma lived, who married a man from Potrero and reported to Grandma, "*No hay más que picardías y groserías aqui—¡y con tantas capillas cerca!*—There's nothing but mischief and bad language around here—and with all these churches nearby!" (She was referring to the fact that the Santuario de Chimayó, the Capilla del Santo Niño, and the Capilla de San Antonio are all located in Potrero.)

"I was up at the capilla, taking pictures," I explain to Juan.

"You better be praying up there, too, and not just taking pictures!" he says, emphatically. And he means it, not so much as a warning but as sage counsel. I make a promise to myself to at least pause for a moment of silence the next time I enter the San Antonio chapel or any other.

Juan is trimming the weeds along the public road because, he says, no one else will do it. He's well into his eighties but still conveys strength and power in his stance and in the casual way he wields the scythe in his hand. He wears a hat emblazoned with the words *Chimayoso Orgulloso* (Proud Chimayoso).

Juan sits on a rock wall beside the road and proceeds to skewer me with insults, and in this he is as eloquent as he is with profanity. "*Me da mucho gusto verlo viniendo, pero me da más gusto verlo salir.*—I'm glad to see you coming, but I'll be happier to see you go," he says. "*Parece muy viejo ya, ¡y ya estás cagando en sus pantalones!*—You look really old, and I'm sure you're already making messes in your pants!" he continues.

Juan tells me about a fight he had recently, when he confronted some youngsters who were drinking and tossing beer cans here. One of them—a good thirty years Juan's junior—threw a punch that hit Juan in the face. "*Pero lo pegé a él dos veces y salió con la cola pa' adentro de las piernas.*—But I hit him back twice, and he ran off with his tail between his legs," Juan says.

He describes for me another altercation that took place a short time ago, when he bested a neighbor in a fistfight over a disagreement about the right-of-way for the Acequia del Potrero. (He's the mayordomo of the acequia and has been for years.) "*¡Le di un chingadazo!*—I gave him a good punch!" he tells me. "*¡Y nunca volvió!*—And he never came back!"

Juan has always been known as a tough character, a stern taskmaster who keeps the ditch running against difficult odds. Sometimes this requires an iron fist, which has earned him the ire of some people.

The door to Juan's house opens, and his dog races out, ripping a quick turn past the Beware of Dog sign and lunging toward me. In a single leap, the small Chihuahua is in Juan's lap, staring into his eyes.

A Chimayó tough guy and his guard dog: neither look so big or bad, as they adore each other. Juan's gruff demeanor is a thin veil over a gentle and warm-hearted soul.

DICHOS ABOUT CHARACTER

Él que es entendido con una vez que le digan, sobra.
    An understanding person only needs to be told only once.

Él que ha de ser barrigón, aunque lo fajan desde chiquito.
    He who is meant to be big bellied will be, even if you bind him when he is little. (You can't change a person's essential nature.)

Él que luce entre las ollas no luce entre las señoras.
    He who shines among the pots doesn't shine among the ladies. (One who dresses up around the house has no good clothes to wear out on the town.)

Él que mal haga, bien no espere.
    One who does something bad should not expect something good in return.

Él que malas mañas tiene, nunca las perderá.
    One who has bad habits will never get rid of them.

Él que nada debe nada teme.
    One who owes nothing fears nothing. (One is who is not guilty fears nothing.)

Él que no llora no mama.
    One who doesn't cry doesn't nurse. (He who doesn't speak up will not get what he wants.)

Él que pronto endienta pronto emparienta.
    An infant who starts teething early will soon have another sibling.

Él que se viste de ajeno, en la calle lo desnudan.
> One who dresses in borrowed clothes will be undressed in the street. (One who lives under false pretenses will be exposed.)

Él que solo se enoja, solo se contenta.
> One who gets mad by himself will have to get over it by himself.

Es como el burro hablando de orejas.
> It's like the burro talking about ears. (Refers to a person talking about what someone else has done when she has committed the same sin.)

Alonzo Trujillo's horse, Los Ojuelos, 2010.

Alonzo's Horses in Los Ojuelos

Más viejo es el aire y todavía sopla.
Much older is the wind, and it still blows.

I'm taking my mother to see Esequiel at his home in the Los Ojuelos neighborhood. We travel along the Arroyo de los Ojuelos and turn to cross the Acequia de la Cañada Ancha, which is running even now, in midwinter. We slip past the charging Rottweiler and into Esequiel's driveway. I tap on the horn, announcing our presence.

Esequiel comes out of his house, a bit taken aback to see my mother's shiny Nissan Infiniti in his yard as he walks over to greet us. He leans in my window to shake my hand and breaks into a grin that widens by a mile when sees Mom.

"*¡Mire no más!*—Will you look at this!" Esequiel exclaims, quickly following with, "Buenas tardes."

He's tickled to see my mother and to recognize her as Benigna's daughter, from the "Ortegas of the Plaza." Mom represents kin from the old days, one of the network of families of the valley who all knew each other—and were all connected to each other—in days gone by. The plática leaps up a notch in energy, because now it involves two people thoroughly versed in the names and places and stories from that fondly remembered past. A rapid-fire exchange of names of relatives and friends, mostly gone, ensues.

But Esequiel has work to do. He points to his son Lorenzo, busy loading up the back of a pickup truck. Lorenzo shouts out a greeting to us but doesn't pause in his labor. Esequiel pulls a woolen watch cap down over his ears and zips a heavy, wool-lined leather jacket against the chilly January air, now cooling quickly as the sun sinks low. He excuses himself and asks if we'll wait for a while, then joins Lorenzo at the idling truck.

Lorenzo dons a white hard hat backward, as if preparing for heavy steel work while keeping a kind of punk style, but the task today at hand is merely filling a blue plastic drum with water from a hose. A couple of hay bales share the bed of the truck with the large, unwieldy barrel. Esequiel, breathing hard as he shoves the slowly filling barrel deeper into the truck, explains to me they're going up the driveway to bring water and the zacate (hay) to the horses. I offer to help, but they have the work well in hand and wave me off.

Within moments the barrel sloshes full, and Esequiel and Lorenzo climb into the cab. The well-worn but carefully maintained four-by-four GMC crawls up the driveway in granny gear, an assortment of dogs trotting behind. We follow in the Infiniti. Esequiel is anxious to finish the chore before the darkness and cold settle in. He nimbly jumps out of the truck at the corrals. The horses shift nervously, especially the edgier white one, who snorts and trots around the enclosure, tail held high. The more timid bay huddles close to the barn, eyeing us thirstily but warily.

Esequiel says he doesn't know the horses' names, and I'm not sure if anyone has ever ridden the skittish, half-wild white one. Esequiel explains that they belong to his son Alonzo, who comes out from Ojo Caliente to care for them but couldn't make it today. As Esequiel maneuvers easily between strands of barbed wire and then through the horizontal poles that define the outer perimeter of the corral, he turns and pulls the wires wide to let me—thirty years his junior—through, apologizing for not having a proper gate.

Lorenzo backs the truck up to the edge of the fencing. He tips the blue barrel over until it rests on the top bar of the corral and water starts to spill out. Esequiel catches the flow in a bucket and hauls it across the corral to a water trough. After several trips back and forth, the barrel drains. Esequiel then tosses the hay out of the truck and uses a plastic snow shovel to carry it over toward the barn. He stops by our car now and then to make a polite comment to my mother, smiling broadly each time. "*O, ese Esequiel es un pedazo de carne bautizada.*—Oh, that Esequiel is a baptized piece of meat," Mom remarks after one such visit, deploying a dicho reserved for an especially kind gentleman.

The corral and the rambling barns and sheds beside it are clearly on their last legs. It's been many decades since they were built. That much is clear, but how they remain standing is a mystery. Many of the *trancas* (horizontal bars) of the corral hang by rusted wire or the merest threads of twine salvaged from hay bales. The two adjacent barns, built of roughhewn logs, lean drunkenly. Their weathered wood, cracked and split, has mellowed to faded tones of gray and rich orange. A sagging door made of rough lumber, held shut with a rusted chain, secures a small shed. A hodgepodge assortment of corrugated metal sheets, some rusted to a dark orange hue and others much newer and still shiny, cover the vigas and rough one-by lumber of the roofs over the rambling structures.

Inside the barn and sheds lie odds and ends and a few bales of hay. The horses can find some shelter in leaning stalls. They pace the corrals, stepping around discarded vigas, trancas, and used pallets. In one corner a junked truck sits, stripped of its motor and most parts.

Behind the barns and corral rise the barrancas that hem in the northern edge of Chimayó. Their vertical cliffs harbor raven nests and offer a roost for pigeons, who coo softly as they look down on Esequiel tending to the horses.

While Esequiel and Lorenzo work on their chores, I pick my way through the corrals, taking pictures of the structures and the animals. The white horse flits nervously, avoiding my every advance, stops, eyes me with a glare conveying a final warning—then breaks into a full gallop, kicking and tearing around the enclosure at a frightening pace, compelling me to back off.

Esequiel pitches hay quickly from the barn into the stalls, then starts to gather up discarded trancas and other scraps of wood. He explains he might as well burn these as firewood, since they're of no use lying around the corral. He tosses a few armloads in the pickup bed. The sun slips closer to the Jémez Mountains as the truck rattles back down the driveway, dogs trailing, and we all scuttle inside Esequiel's house. It's warm and fragrant with piñón smoke. Esequiel puts a kettle of water on a worn woodstove to make coffee for Mom and me.

As the water warms toward a boil, we get to talking about Esequiel's favorite subject: his tenure as the leader of the Matachines in Chimayó. He offers to show me his dance costumes.

"*Pero tenemos que apurar.*—But we have to hurry," he says. "*Ya mero se mete el sol.*—The sun is about to set."

"*Está como dos en un zapato.*—He is like two in one shoe," Mom says, meaning that he's anxious to get going. While she waits in the cozy kitchen, Esequiel grabs a key from a nail in the kitchen doorjamb and leads me through the sala, past an enormous drum made from a giant cottonwood trunk and rawhide (the one he promised to show me). A television glows above the drum, which serves now as a coffee table. He points with his chin and says, "*Allí está el tambor.—* There's the drum," and we hurry through the room. We exit the house through the front door, an entrance that is hardly ever used. Outside, Esequiel labors to shove aside a wooden cabinet blocking the door to a small room adjoining the porch. He's placed the heavy cabinet there to make it difficult to break in.

Esequiel turns the key in the lock, opens the door, and beckons me into an unheated, unlighted room crammed with furniture, boxes, an old TV, and other items no longer in use. In the dim light my eyes are drawn to a dozen Matachín coronas (crowns) that emblazon the back wall with their multicolored ribbons. Their vibrancy contrasts with the dull, dusty gray of all the discarded household goods. Nearby, an American flag rolled up around a pole offers another splash of color in the drab room.

Esequiel unhooks the largest headdress and brings it toward me. For better light, we step out through the porch and then into the house, where Esequiel holds it up by the large picture window.

"*Esta corona la hizo mi papá.—*My father made this crown," he says, and as he turns the piece slowly, I'm stunned by its very presence. Multicolored beads looped extravagantly around it shimmer. Ribbons dangle and twirl lightly. While he holds a Matachín *palma* (trident) in his left hand and the corona in his right, Esequiel talks about this, his personal headpiece, the most magnificent of the lot he keeps in the room. He was the monarca in the dances, the leader who represents Montezuma, the last Aztec king. His corona befits the role. Its glow seems to intensify as the light fades, a sacred object, made so by its antiquity, its association with such a venerable dance, and by Esequiel's reverence and love for everything the dance represents. His presentation is all the more poignant for me because I realize that Esequiel may be the end of the line for its practitioners in Chimayó.

Esequiel again talks reverently, as he did at Magdalena's last spring, about the many times he danced. He's still hopeful his niece will take up the mantle and keep the dances alive in Chimayó. But he hurries as dusk falls to place the corona back with the others in the dusty storeroom. He locks the door and slides the heavy cabinet back into place, and we reenter the warmth of the house. He's anxious about my waiting mother, who is ready to go home to Santa Fe. We'll come back again to see the rest of the coronas when we have more time.

Esequiel Trujillo and his corona, *Los Ojuelos, 2009.*

DICHOS ABOUT CHARACTER

Él que duerme en casa ajena, de mañana se levanta, limpiándose la lagaña y a ver pa' dónde arranca.
> He who sleeps in someone else's home gets up early, wipes the sleep out of his eyes, and looks to see where to go. (Sleeping in a strange house leaves one disoriented and unrested.)

Él que solo se ríe, de sus maldades se acuerda.
> One who is laughing to himself is remembering the mischievous things he has done.

Él que temprano se moja, tiempo tiene de secarse.
> One who bathes early has time to dry himself. (Get ready early so you can have time to get to work.)

Él que todo lo quiere todo lo pierde.
> One who wants all loses everything. (Said of greedy people.)

Es amigo de San Dame pero de San Toma, no.
> He is a friend of Saint Give to Me but not of Saint Give to Another. (He's stingy.)

Es como el perro del hortelano, ni deja, ni deja comer.
> She is like the farmer's dog—she neither leaves food nor lets anyone else eat. (Said of a stingy person.)

Es en contra de la corriente.
> She goes against the current. (Said of a contrary person.)

Es más lo que habla que lo que dice.
> He talks more than he says. (He uses many words to say little of meaning.)

Es tan vivo que todo lo que le dan se come.
> She is so smart that everything they feed her she will eat. (Said of someone who thinks she is smart but is gullible.)

Es un pedazo de carne bautizado.
> He is a baptized piece of meat. (Said of an especially kind person.)

Es un santito con cuernos.
> He is a little saint with horns. (Said of a person who pretends to be good but isn't.)

Santos Ortiz's burned house near the Plaza del Cerro, 2010.

Santos Ortiz's House

No le busques pies al gato porque le hallas cuatro.
Don't go looking for the cat's feet, because you will find four.

I'm in Chimayó to photograph a crumbling adobe wall. I first stumbled across it on Christmas day, when my brother and I took a break from family festivities at my sister's house nearby to go looking for good light for painting. Arturo is a painter, and he is always searching out the "magic hour" light. It's a quest I share with him. On Christmas, we looped around the old plaza road just as the low winter sun was casting its last golden rays on the worn, pastel-hued patina of the adobe wall, the remnants of a house that had burned down a few years before. I couldn't assemble my camera gear quickly enough to catch the golden light then and vowed to revisit the wall on another clear winter evening soon.

It's just over a week later and I'm back, with plenty of time before sunset to place my tripod and choose an angle for the magic hour light. But I have a problem. New, tightly strung barbed wire—a rarity in Chimayó—blocks access to the field. I have to get inside in order to find the right perspective on the wall, but I don't know who owns the land. Were it a fallen fence on property whose owner I knew, I might act differently. But I'm reluctant to cross the boundary now. My friends Chris and Nancy live nearby, and I think to ask them who owns this property. But their gate is closed and locked. So I drive toward the next nearest house.

On my way down the road, I remember the first time I passed this way, many years ago. It is only a few hundred yards from the Plaza del Cerro, but back then, when I was seven years old, this was well outside my zone of comfort in Chimayó. And to put me even more ill at ease on that distant day, I was actually driving a car. It was the 1932 Chevy that had been parked for decades in the garage of my great-grandpa's *dispensa* (storage building) next door to Grandma's house. Arturo and I had rolled the car out of the driveway while Grandma and Mom were busy inside. Arturo, seven years my senior, had managed to finagle the keys for our family car, a 1962 Dodge station wagon, and was determined to start the old Chevy by pulling it down the road with the newer Dodge and "popping the clutch."

So I found myself behind the wheel of the giant old car, a marvel of gleaming black steel and chrome, straining to reach the pedals and see over the hood as we bumped along at twenty miles an hour. I was trying to keep clear Arturo's instructions. He was most emphatic in telling me to push down the brake pedal if I saw the Dodge's red brake lights go on. That much I was sure of, but I didn't really understand how to let go of the clutch, hit the gas, and rev the engine when he gave me a hand signal.

We wanted to stay away from houses and the prying eyes of neighbors, and so Arturo pulled me (using an old strap we'd found in the dispensa) down through the plaza, in front of Tía Melita and Uncle Ike's house, and down around this corner, past the two-story adobe house whose burned and partially fallen wall I want to photograph now.

When Arturo made the hand signal to let go of the clutch, I did—but the engine didn't catch. I jammed the clutch back to the floor, which made my head sink below the level of the steering wheel, but not before I saw we were rapidly running out of road. Just ahead was the T-junction with the dirt track in "the first arroyo," and as we drew near, the taillights on the Dodge lit up. But I could barely see above the hood of the Chevy, and in any case Arturo's instructions about the gas and clutch and brake pedals all merged in my mind. I did nothing, and the Chevy slammed into the back of our new family car. I still remember the look of astonishment on Arturo's face when he emerged to survey the damage. The tailgate of the car was deeply dented, but the Chevy, solid as a tank, had suffered no harm.

The thrill of that ride could never be repeated. It was like riding a spirited horse, someone else's horse, a feeling expressed by the dicho "*Caballo ajeno, espuelas propias: el mundo es mío.*—Borrowed horse, my own spurs: the world is mine."

But I'm back in the 'hood now and turning into the driveway of a house whose owner I don't know at all. I roll up to the drive port and beep the horn.

A young man comes out, looking perplexed as he circles around to my window. I introduce myself and tell him who my family is. He is nonplussed by this information; he's too young to have heard of my kin in the plaza, most of whom are dead.

"I'm wondering if you know who owns that property with the burned-out adobe on it," I say. He looks even more confused and more than a little suspicious. I explain I'm taking photographs around Chimayó, especially of old buildings, and that the wall in early evening light would make a really nice picture.

"It reminds me of an old Greek ruin or something," I say by way of explanation, and although his bewilderment doesn't diminish, he tells me the ruin belongs to a "some guy who lives out of state." Then he comes closer and asks, "Have you seen anyone walking around here, anyone suspicious looking?"

I'm taken aback by his anxious expression, but his question brings to mind three teenagers I passed just as I exited the old plaza on my way down here. With baggy pants, tattoos, shaved heads, and a cocky kind of strut, they might be considered suspicious looking, although I'm not one to profile. They did give me the friendly—or at least nonthreatening—Chimayó nod, a quick up-flip of the chin that passes for a "howdy." But I know the history of at least one of the kids, and that doesn't weigh in his favor. So I tell the man in the driveway about them. He shakes his head and describes a shattered window and footprints in the snow behind his home.

I'm no stranger to burglary. Just about everyone has suffered a break-in in Chimayó at least once, and there are countless stories about the audacity of the thieves, some of them told and retold because of their almost comical nature. I recall when someone broke into Tío Victor's store on the Plaza del Cerro and made off with all the merchandise that was left there after Victor's death in 1945. They say that after the break-in people showed up at the post office wearing the old-fashioned button-up shoes that had been lifted. Then there was the time that someone made the mistake of breaking into the trailer of a man who kept a tiger and other exotic cats in his home; the burglar escaped but showed up at the hospital with a mutilated leg.

The yarns about Chimayó burglaries go on and on with their dark humor, and in general people remain vigilant about that kind of crime at all times—a sad fact that has spawned a modern-day bilingual *dicho* of sorts, uttered by an aged cousin of mine as she took leave from a family gathering: "*Ya tengo que irme a mi casa, antes de que hagan* break-in.—I have to go home now, before they commit a break-in."

Crime waves come and go in Chimayó. A particularly dramatic peak in the mid-1990s inspired local citizens to form an organization, the Chimayó Crime Prevention Association, to do something to slow down the rash of burglaries that was plaguing the valley. At one point the organization, which included business owners and citizens of every stripe, held a meeting in the parish hall of the Holy Family Church. Residents vented their frustration with representatives of law enforcement agencies and the courts—and with each other. One woman stood up to shout at a man across the room, accusing him of stealing her television just the night before. A crazily drunk man complained that he was stopped by officers who had the nerve to "take the law into their own hands" as they arrested him on outstanding warrants and suspicion of driving under the influence of alcohol. (He got no sympathy from the crowd.)

The hard work and persistence of the crime prevention group led to significant improvement in law enforcement. Federal, state, and local law enforcement officers descended on Chimayó by air and land one Sunday morning, mounting a major bust that cleared out several drug dealers, including some who had been entrenched in the community for decades. The Santa Fe newspaper published a map showing the locations of the major drug dealers' houses (a nice map that I copied and used to give directions to my house, which was near one of the homes busted in the sweep). This slowed down the traffic to the dealers' homes, and burglaries, which are almost all committed by addicts stealing goods to sell to feed their habits, dipped dramatically.

As I look at the angry expression on his face before me, I commiserate with the recent crime victim and ask him what he lost in the burglary.

"Just my gun," he says, "and the TV."

The homeowner's brother roars up in his pickup, and then my friend Chris, who lives nearby, walks up. They've heard about the break-in and are here to find out what happened. After some talk about the crime at hand, I tell Chris about my desire to find the owner of the property across the road. He knows who it is and assures me it's OK to cross the fence and take photographs, but he'll call the owner in Florida to be sure.

I climb over the shiny new wire and drop into the property where the wall stands. The house that stood here belonged to Santos Ortiz, an industrious *vecino* who had seven children and put them all to work in various enterprises, including weaving. Each child had a job in the family corporation; one cooked, one did dishes, one fed and cared for the animals, one spun wool, a few wove, and so on. He was a stern taskmaster and turned a handy profit—enough for him to build the first two-story adobe in Chimayó, which people came to marvel at. I'm looking at fragments of its tall walls now.

The Ortiz family name has been around for a long time and has many ties to other families in the Plaza del Cerro area. Our family papers first record the name in 1820, when Matías Ortiz signed as a witness to a land sale from Pascual and Nicolás Ortega to Manuel Ortega, my great-great-great-great-grandfather.

There are patches of snow on the ground, and the evening chill is settling. Deep magenta light is already starting to creep across the landscape and onto the plaster of the burned adobe walls. There is little time, so I begin positioning myself, searching for the best angle on the crumbling structure that stands in the weedy field.

The sound of footsteps on the crusty snow behind me surprises me. I spin around to see a young man bent low over the ground, examining something intently. I shout a startled greeting, and he barely acknowledges my presence, then kneels in the snow and reaches down again. Looking closer, I see a tape measure in his hand. He's measuring my footprints. It dawns on me that he's investigating the crime scene, comparing the size of my prints to those found along the back wall of the house, beneath the broken window.

Of course I would be a prime suspect. I'm a stranger here, and the break-in happened moments before I showed up. I hope my shoe size doesn't match the size of the burglar's. But there's no time for distractions. The wall stands in full, radiant winter sunlight. Framing it from multiple angles as the sun drops behind the mountains occupies me until darkness falls.

DICHOS ABOUT CHARACTER

Es una lámpara que da luz sin aceite.
    She is lamp that gives light without oil. (Said of a very smart person.)

Ese huevo quiere sal.
    That egg wants salt. (Said when a person is especially nice because he wants something.)

Está a migajas de otro.
    He is at the mercy of others.

Está como dos en un zapato.
    He is like two in one shoe. (He's anxious to get going.)

Gente melosa, siempre cautelosa.
    With sweet people, always be cautious.

Habiendo carne y cueva aunque llueva.
    If one has meat and a cave to stay in, it doesn't matter if it rains.
    (If your basic needs are met, the problems of the world are of little consequence.)

Hacen más unos callando que otros gritando.
    There are those who accomplish more being quiet than others who are shouting.

Hay muertos que no hacen ruido, y son mayores sus penas.
>There are dead people who don't make noise, and their woes are greater. (Said of people who go about quietly committing sins worse than those committed by people who do not hide their actions.)

La caridad bien ordenada empieza por uno mismo.
>Charity well dispensed starts with oneself.

La mona, aunque se vista de seda, mona se queda.
>Even if she dresses in silk, a monkey is still a monkey.

Perro que ladra no muerde.
>A dog that barks doesn't bite. (His bark is bigger than his bite.)

Aaron Martínez and his truck, Los Ranchos, 2010.

Aaron Martínez in Los Ranchos

En la conformidad está la felicidad.
Agreement brings happiness.

We came to Chimayó today without expectations, and we're dazzled by apricot blossoms glowing brightly against a cracked adobe wall on a small tree near the plaza. This beleaguered tree greets the spring against all odds. No one planted it; it probably sprouted from a discarded pit, and it gets water only at the whim of rainfall. The fruit will bud as the flowers fade, but it will almost certainly freeze in the next few weeks. And the building beside it—no one has plastered it in years, and it may not even be standing next year.

After I take many photographs of the blossoms against the cracked walls, Mom and I stop in at Ortega's Weaving Shop, right across the road from Grandma's house. When I stayed in Chimayó in the summers, I would wake every morning to the sound of the big looms banging away as David Ortega and his brother Joe turned out blankets. As a teenager, I worked at the weaving shop, making 26-by-42-inch and, later, 36-by-60-inch rugs. David and his sons Robert and Andrew taught me to weave, although it's been long in our family. David's father, Nicasio, was my great-grandfather Reyes's younger brother. Reyes opened a weaving shop in Chimayó first, in 1900, although he had been weaving for dealers in Santa Fe (principally Jesusito Candelaria) for years. Tío Nicasio followed by opening his own weaving shop across from Reyes's, and the two competed for the rare tourist who came up the road from Española.

I have many fine pieces from Reyes, and one from his father, José Ramón Ortega y Vigil, that must have been woven in the 1880s—a beautiful striped piece made of hand-spun and -dyed wool. I also have blankets woven by my grandfather Abedón Chávez, who learned from my grandmother how to weave and became one of the best weavers in Chimayó. In fact, David Ortega always said that Abedón was the best weaver he had ever known.

As we're talking about old family weavings, Robert takes us downstairs to show us one he's recently acquired, a large rug bearing a thunderbird design in the center, with thunderbolts and swastikas in the borders. It was woven by my grandpa Reyes prior to World War II, before swastikas as symbols became synonymous with evil. In Reyes's time, the swastika was one of a number of symbols associated with Native American culture, and, like other such symbols, it was used in Hispanic arts to give them a kind of Native American cachet. (The swastika was a sacred symbol in many cultures worldwide before the Nazis appropriated it.) A customer gave the rug to Robert, saying that his grandparents had bought it from Reyes.

After chatting with Robert and his brother Andrew, who owns the Galería Ortega next door, we get back in the car and drive down to "the second arroyo," not far from the old plaza, on a road Mom knew well in her youth. ("We don't have street names here; we go by arroyos," she reminds me.) We want to call on Alicia Martínez, an old family friend whom we haven't seen for some years, but it's proving difficult to pick out her house from the maze of newer homes and trailers. Most of the old houses Mom knew as landmarks are gone, and we wouldn't think of calling Alicia to tell her we were coming or to ask directions; that would be outside of the etiquette of visiting in Chimayó.

This part of Chimayó is known as Los Ranchos, a common moniker among New Mexico place-names that means "the farms." If a plaza ever stood here, it has long since vanished, although there apparently once was a chapel here dedicated to San Joaquín. A will left by José Antonio Cruz in 1837 mentions a small room, three vigas wide, dedicated to his patron saint, *"mi padre mio San Juaquin."* There is a morada still standing here and in use by a handful of Hermanos, but it is dedicated primarily to El Señor de Esquipulas.

Looking in vain in Los Ranchos for Alicia's home and any sign of the old plaza, we spot someone stepping out of a garage and walking toward a house set back a distance from the road. I flag him down.

"¡Oiga! Ando buscando la casa de Alicia Martínez.—Hey! I'm looking for Alicia Martínez's house," I call out.

Morada, Los Ranchos, ca. 1990.

The man turns and calls back, "*Queda más por este rumbo.*—It's farther down that way," pointing down the road.

Then recognition dawns for both of us. I knew Aaron years back, when I interviewed his mother, Cordelia, in 1990 for my first Chimayó book, *Sabino's Map: Life in Chimayó's Old Plaza*. He walks over and leans in the window to greet my mother. The conversation resumes, now in English, as I introduce Aaron.

"Oh, hi. Of course I know who you are, but I don't know if we've met," Aaron says, assuming a more formal tone when he addresses Mom. "I'm Cordelia and Estevan's son."

"Yes, I remember Estevan, from the plaza—José Inez's son. He was our relative somehow. My mother always called him 'primo José Inez,'" Mom answers.

"It was through the Ortegas," Aaron explains.

"The Ortegas? How is that?"

"On my father's side," Aaron continues. "My grandfather was second cousin to José Ramón Ortega—"

"My great-grandpa," Mom interjects.

"Yes, my father's grandmother, María Antonia Ortega—José Ramón's sister—was married to Concepción Trujillo, of Río Chiquito," Aaron continues. "And on the other side, my other grandfather's father, Crístobal Martínez, married a daughter of Pedro Asencio Ortega."

"Really? Pedro Asencio was Grabiel Ortega's son. That goes way back," my mother offers, alluding to the fact that Grabiel Ortega was the first Ortega to settle in Chimayó, in the early 1700s. "But I remember now we also were related to your mother, Cordelia. Her father, Torbio Trujillo, was brother to Severiano and Nicolás. Severiano married Seniada Ortega, my grandpa's sister, so we were connected that way, through marriage."

I am quickly losing track of who is who.

"That's right," Aaron goes on, "but it goes back farther on that side, too. María Francisca Ortega, who was born in 1797 to José Manuel Pablo Ortega and Ana María Gonzales, married José del Carmen Trujillo. Their son was José Concepción Trujillo from Rincón—not to be confused with the José Concepción Trujillo from Río Chiquito. Their son Toribio was my mother's father.

"And actually, Severiano—who, like you said, married your great-aunt, Senaida—was only half brother to Toribio. See, Toribio's mother was Chonita Coriz; Severiano's mother was Josefa Pacheco. Chonita came from Santa Fe as a girl to be a servant in Josefa and José Concepción's house. After Josefa died, Concepción married the servant, Chonita—my grandpa Toribio's mother."

"I didn't know that," Mom comments, and at this point I am completely lost in the Gordian knot and don't even know what she doesn't know. "I just knew we were related to the Trujillos of Rincón through Severiano. We considered Severiano's brothers, including Toribio, Nicolás, and others, to be tíos. We didn't know Toribio was a half brother to them," Mom adds.

"Toribio had ten half brothers in all and only one sister," Aaron explains. "I found out by studying the genealogy."

"Anyway," Mom concludes, "that's why my mother called your grandfather 'primo José Inez.'"

"Then for sure we're cousins," I finally chime in, making the only statement I'm certain of.

Aaron is restoring a 1952 Ford pickup he keeps in the garage. He swings open the doors to show it to us. It leers from the darkness, a chrome and steel behemoth reeking of gasoline and oil. Aaron tells us this was his father's truck and that he intends to paint it and overhaul the engine in the coming year. He's retired from his job in Los Alamos but still lives there. He was in the habit of visiting his mother, Cordelia, in Chimayó. But she's passed on, and he comes now to maintain the house and fiddle with the old truck. It's like this with so many people in Chimayó who have moved away, including us with our family land and houses: having property gives us an excuse to visit and, while we're at it, to reconnect with family roots, to remember the old days, and to retouch the earth—or the old machinery.

Leaving the Second Arroyo and Aaron behind, Mom and I cross through the Plaza del Cerro and then take Baca's Road up past the Presbyterian cemetery. We're coming this way so she can confirm for me the location of a landmark mentioned in a document we have, dated April 18, 1766. That paper, a petition by Antonia Lopes for a division of land, refers to a *piedra azul* (blue rock outcropping) at the edge of the mountains: "*por lindero una peña azul que está a la margen del serro de parte de horiente.*—for a boundary a blue rock that is on the edge of the hill on the east part."

Mom was able to connect this description with a place she used to go in her childhood to get a view of the Chimayó Valley, and she wants to show it to me. The rock outcrop stands almost precisely at the boundary between two parcels of land—probably the same parcels divided in Antonia Lopes's petition. I think it marks the first division of the land grant given by the Spanish Crown to Luis López in 1706, which López sold to Grabiel Ortega.

I park at the Presbyterian cemetery, and Mom points out the rock outcropping. Sure enough, it's blue, and it sits at the edge of the foothills. Glancing back down toward the plaza along the fence line stretching westward from the rock, I wonder what this view looked like when Antonia Lopes made her claim for land in the sparsely settled valley 245 years ago, almost to the day.

DICHOS ABOUT CHARACTER

Le entra por un oído y le sale por el otro.
    It goes in one ear and comes out the other.

Le está haciendo falta la fiesta del Quemado.
    He is missing the feast from Quemado. (Said of someone who was mooching off of other people, but now they cut him off.)

Le falta un real para el peso y la mitad de la semana.
    He is a quarter short of a dollar and half of the week. (He is daft.)

Le falta un tornillo.
    He's missing a screw. (He is daft.)

Le ofrecen almohada y quiere colchón.
    They offer him a pillow, and he wants a mattress. (They offer him an inch and he wants a mile.)

Lo que sobra reparte.
    She shares the leftovers. (She gives only what she doesn't want anymore; she's stingy.)

Mal de muchos, consuelo de tontos.
    The suffering of many is the consolation of fools.

Más altas están las nubes y el aire las desbarata.
    As high as the clouds are, the wind still scatters them. (No matter how high a position you reach in life, you can fall.)

Más hace él que quiere que él que puede.
>   The person who wants to do something does more than the one who can do it but won't.

Más sabe el loco en su casa que el sabio en la ajena.
>   A crazy man knows more in his own house than a wise man in someone else's.

Oratorio de San Buenaventura San Buenaventura, Plaza del Cerro, ca. 1995.

El Oratorio de San Buenaventura

El diablo no duerme.
The devil doesn't sleep.

The peach trees are in bloom as we approach Magdalena Espinosa's house. The noonday sun shines down on the brilliant blossoms, made all the more striking because the tree stands beside her bright turquoise-blue garage door.

We've heard Magdalena's health is failing and want to pay a visit. It's been a half year since our memorable time with her and Esequiel here. But April is the cruelest month, as T. S. Eliot said, and it seems to me to be truer every spring. It's not likely Magdalena will last out the change in season, and we aren't meant to see her today to say our farewells. She's slipping away and is already inaccessible to us.

Mom and I drive away from La Cuchilla in the somber spring sunlight and decide to visit the oratorio, the small chapel dedicated to San Buenaventura, which for many decades was the center of community celebration and mourning on the Plaza del Cerro. But on the way I detour down a little-used road to show Mom an even humbler site, a small shrine in a field. It's a simple structure, perhaps six feet tall, made of concrete painted white and roofed with fiberglass pinned down by river rocks. A defunct red Toyota is parked up against one of the shrine's crumbling walls.

Blue trim borders the opening of the sanctuary, framing an interior space filled with religious paraphernalia: prints of the Virgin Mary; votive candles bearing images of Christ, Mary, and several saints; and a calendar adorned with an image of the Virgin of Guadalupe and a devotional prayer. Strings of Christmas lights, plastic strands of evergreen boughs, and other ornaments are draped over and around these items. The newness of some of the objects reveals the place is visited frequently, even though it is weathering away.

Seeking access beyond the fence to get closer to the shrine, I knock on the door of the house nearby. No response. I'm waiting when a large, jacked-up four-wheel-drive truck pulls up, its windows darkly tinted. The door opens, and a woman in a black dress steps down to a gleaming chrome step, then to the ground. Perhaps in her midseventies, she has lustrous, raven-black hair. Fine crow's-feet dance around her bright green eyes, the only wrinkles in her otherwise smooth bronze skin; they add a touch of elegance to her graceful demeanor. She smiles and beams a look that utterly enchants me. Her daughter and son-in-law exit the truck and join her in greeting me. They're all delighted I would like to photograph their little shrine, but the woman refuses me a picture of herself. No amount of charm in Spanish or English can sway her.

I spend a few minutes at the shrine, and, mindful of the admonition I had received from Juan Trujillo to be sure to pray when visiting holy places, I pause for a moment of silence. Mom watches from the car. A prayer I learned from her and Grandma comes to me:

Con Jesús me acuesto
Con Jesús me levanto
Con la virgen María y el Espíritu Santo . . .

And along with that comes a joke both Grandma and Mom used to tell. It goes something like this:

It seems there was a young man in the plaza who wasn't quite right in the head. (When he or similar characters came up in conversation, Grandma had several dichos at hand, such as "*Le falta un real para el peso y la mitad de la semana*—He is a quarter short of a dollar and half of the week" or "*Le falta un tornillo.*—He's missing a screw." Mostly, though, she would characterize such unfortunate souls as *medio medio*.) One night as he and his mother knelt to pray, they recited the prayer I just recalled, which translates as:

"With Jesus I lay down to rest
With Jesus I rise
With the Virgin Mary and the Holy Spirit—"

At which point the young man interjected: "*¡Embustera! ¡Se acuesta con papá y se levanta con él también!*—Liar! You lay down with Dad, and you get up with him, too!"

When Grandma told this little story, she would conclude with the dicho "*¡Los locos y los chiquitos dicen la verdad!*—Crazy people and little children tell the truth!"

My laughter beside the shrine isn't exactly the kind of reverence Juan Trujillo had hoped for when he lectured me, but it somehow doesn't seem inappropriate. Mom and I share a good giggle over the old joke as we drive away toward the Oratorio de San Buenaventura at the Plaza del Cerro.

It strikes me that in all the times I've visited the capilla on the Plaza del Cerro, I've only entered once with my mother—on the day the priest blessed the new bell we had painstakingly installed. Now it's just the two of us here, and the plaza is extraordinarily quiet. I open the padlock securing the door and help Mom step up into the dark, cool interior of the capilla. An even greater stillness envelops us.

The oratorio is not a freestanding structure like other capillas in the valley. It's simply one of the many rooms comprising the perimeter of the Plaza del Cerro, a room dedicated by Pedro Ascencio Ortega to the patron saint of the Plaza del Cerro, San Buenaventura. A small bulto (statue) of the santo patrón—a replacement for the stolen original—presides over the silence, his figure ensconced in a recess at the center of an elegant *retablo de altar* (altar screen) painted by one of nineteenth-century New Mexico's most prolific and well-known santeros, Rafael Aragón. Although the plaza wasn't built until the 1780s or so, people in this part of the valley had been devoted to San Buenaventura long before. Some of the early documents in our collection mention Buenaventura as the santo patrón of the area. Indeed, a 1758 land sale and the 1766 paper dividing the land of Antonia Lopes—the one mentioning the blue rock—calls this part of the valley "*el partido de San Buena Bentura*—the jurisdiction of San Buenaventura."

San Buenaventura, whose feast day is July 15, is an uncommon figure in the iconography of northern New Mexico. His reputation in the Catholic world resides more in his intellectual appeal than in supernatural powers. People do not petition him for a specific kind of intercession. Rather, he is recognized as a great scholar and mystic and an early, central figure in the Franciscan order. I often wonder why he was chosen as the patron saint of this small plaza. In New Mexico, he is the patron saint of few places, among them Cochití Pueblo and the abandoned Las Humanas mission. Perhaps he was chosen because the plaza was founded on his feast day, but there is no document that gives a date.

Mom sits quietly in the oratorio on a sagging bench fashioned of roughhewn boards joined without nails. Above her, handmade *arañas* (simple wooden chandeliers) hang motionless in the still air, their candles reduced to lumps of wax that haven't been molten for many years. She studies the altar screen, the dusty linen on the altar, the carved figure of San Buenaventura, secure in its small *nicho*.

Pedro Asencio Ortega's will describes in detail the contents of this room, which at the time of his death was one of the rooms in his house. He enumerates items in the chapel, including one of the arañas hanging from the ceiling. (A cousin of mine held the original copy of Ortega's will, but it seems to have been lost.)

"Look, the banners of the Carmelitas are still here," she says, pointing to the plastic-shrouded standards leaning in the corners, each emblazoned with the name of the women's confraternity that used to maintain this place: Cofradía de Nuestra Señora del Carmen—the Confraternity of Our Lady of Mount Carmel. One includes a supplication: *Ruega por nosotros.*—Pray for us.

I'm not sure why the Carmelitas, as the women's group used to be called, chose this capilla for their meeting place. It would seem the chapel dedicated to Señora del Carmen, in La Cuchilla, would have been the more natural choice. But for many decades the Carmelitas held their meetings here and each May led the plaza residents in a celebration of the Mes de María, the Month of Mary.

"I was a flower girl for the Carmelitas when they walked around the plaza saying the rosary," Mom says, recalling the annual procession on the last day of May. "Tila and Urbanita and all the little girls and I would go up in the hills and along the ditches to gather flowers, and then we'd walk ahead of the women and throw the flowers on the path in front of them. We felt very special having a role to play in the procession."

The Carmelitas maintained the oratorio for most of the twentieth century, led by my great-grandfather's spinster sister, Bonefacia Ortega. (As expressed in the dicho for a woman who never marries, "*Se quedó para vestir santos.*—She was left to dress the saints.") She was one of a long line of Ortegas to take a leadership role in maintaining the oratorio. But in fact the care for the place has always been a community affair. We have notes from the late 1800s listing the names of people who contributed *limosnas*, or alms, for the upkeep of the place.

For their contributions, most offered *dos reales* (a quarter) or ten or twenty cents; but some didn't have money and instead offered a handful of tobacco, a half a ristra of chile, a fanega (roughly a bushel) of wheat, or a couple of almudes (half fanegas) of *alverjones* (chickpeas).

In a license issued in 1860, Archbishop "Juan B. Lamy" (i.e., Jean-Baptiste Lamy, the first archbishop of Santa Fe) authorized the Carmelitas to collect alms. Among our papers is a handwritten copy of the original document, penned by Juan de Jesús Trugillo, the priest in Santa Cruz de la Cañada.

The plaza community contributed to the upkeep of the chapel in many ways. Looking up to the ceiling made of hand-split pine boards, I note the signatures of men who helped renovate the place in 1873. Notably absent are women's names, even though they certainly contributed to the work. In those days, women usually took charge of the plastering, and they probably fed the men working on the roof as well.

The oratorio occasionally served as a place for meetings of Los Hermanos. It may, in fact, originally have been created as a formal morada. Although the architecture of moradas varies from community to community, many of them are bipartite in layout, with one section devoted to everyday activities and the other, called an oratorio, reserved for prayer, singing, and the other Hermanos rituals. (The Hermanos are best known for performing rituals during Holy Week, although the organization serves many other social functions as well.) Pedro Asencio Ortega married Bernardo Abeyta's daughter. Bernardo was the patron who built the santuario and also was renowned as an hermano mayor in the brotherhood. Pedro Asencio's son José Ramón Ortega y Abeyta served in the brotherhood and took care of the oratorio. Furthermore, the Carmelitas were closely affiliated with Los Hermanos, acting as a female counterpart to the men's group and assisting with many its activities. All this makes me wonder if the oratorio originally was a meeting place for Los Hermanos.

Mom reads the names on the ceiling aloud.

"Jose Patricio Trujillo . . . Jose Pantalion Jaramillo . . . Jose Candelario Trugillo . . . Jose Guadalupe Ortega . . . Jose Eugenio Martines . . . Jose Livio Ortega . . . Jose Agapito Ortega . . . Jose Anastasio Jaramillo . . . Jose Antonio Martines . . ."

To his signature, José Antonio Martines added the notation: "*En el año de 1873 se renebo la casa de San Buena Bentura.*—In the year of 1873, the house of San Buenaventura was renovated."

Mom is very well versed in the genealogy of the plaza families, but even so she can't connect all of the names with lineages she knows. She does place Agapito, though.

"Oh, Agapito—that was Doña Socorro's husband—remember him? Socorro was Trinidad's mother. Trinidad Ortega was married to Eufelia. They lived right across the road from Tía Melita. I remember Socorro. She was from the generation of the old-timers who were around when I was little."

Recalling one of the documents in the family collection, I ask, "Remember the letter from Domingo Ortega to his father, Gerbacio? He was writing home from Conejos, Colorado, announcing the birth of a daughter, María Petra del Socorro? Is that Agapito's wife?"

"No, Doña Socorro was not related to us," Mom answers. "María Petra del Socorro was Domingo Ortega's daughter. They eventually settled in Mora. Doña Socorro was Ortega because of her marriage to Agapito Ortega, who was related to that other branch of the Ortegas—not ours—some way. *Era harina de otro costal.*—She was flour from another sack," Mom says, citing a dicho.

The names on the ceiling and on the lists of almsgivers offer snapshots of who lived here in the late nineteenth century, before Protestant missionaries showed up to challenge the religious orthodoxy of the plaza. Soon after the arrival of the first minister, the caretaker of the oratorio, José Ramón Ortega y Abeyta (not to be confused with his neighbor, my ancestor José Ramón Ortega y Vigil), converted to Protestantism and handed over the keys to the oratorio to Tía Bonefacia, sometime around 1900. The Reformation had come to Chimayó.

We sit quietly in the oratorio for some time, immersed in the peculiar, solemn spell that always envelops it. Mom reminds me that at least one of our relatives rests here, buried in the dirt floor beneath our feet. One of the papers Mom keeps names the child, Gumersinda Ortega, who died in 1909 at the age of three. Grandma mentioned her often, along with the names of the other deceased siblings in her family: Corina, Antonio, Sabinita. Children were often buried here in the oratorio, as this was considered holy ground, suitable for interring children who died without the benefit of last rites. The sanctified ground would secure the *angelitos*' passage to join the celestial saints whose visages watch over this place.

We study the fine strokes in Aragón's retablo and the simplicity and elegance of the small religious prints on the walls, hung in handworked tin frames at random intervals here and there. The plain white walls, the dark steel woodstove,

Interior, Oratorio de San Buenaventura, 2009.

the wooden railing in front of the altar—everything here bespeaks a powerful but humble piety and a careful attention to maintaining an atmosphere of sacredness.

The only jarring element in the tranquil and perfectly composed scene is the severed rope that was connected to the bell now absent from the crooked belfry on top of the oratorio. The rope lies on a bench where it fell when the thieves cut it and pitched the heavy bell off the roof—no easy feat and one that took considerable determination to pull off. The limp, crudely cut rope with a loop on one end lies there like a used hangman's noose. This violation of sacred space and the spirit of community is a pitiful reminder of the tragic decline of this plaza. The oratorio is still here, looking almost exactly as it did 150 years ago, but we're none too sure how many more it will last.

And we've heard that lately a nearby resident has been gleefully ringing a bell in his backyard, his delight apparent in the loud laughter accompanying the peals.

DICHOS ABOUT CHARACTER

Me dijo del paladar al diente.
    She spoke to me from the palate to the tooth. (Said when somebody tells you something they don't really mean.)

Me quiere jugar un dos por cuatro.
    He wants to give me two for four. (He wants to cheat me.)

Me quiere tapar el sol con la mano.
    He wants to cover the sun with his hand. (He wants to make a fool out of me.)

Me siento como cabra en corral ajeno.
    I feel like a goat in someone else's corral. (I feel out of place.)

Muerto el perro, se acaba la rabia.
    The rabies is gone after the dog is dead. (When a person dies, his anger dies with him.)

No es el león como lo pintan.
    The lion is not the way they paint him to be.

No hay peor sordo que él que no quiere oír.
    There is no deaf person worse than one who doesn't want to hear.

No le esconde la vela a nadie.
    She will not hide the candle for anyone. (Said of someone who can't keep a secret.)

No hay celos en Margarita.
> There is no jealousy in Margaret. (Said when someone doesn't mind what another is doing because she is guilty of doing the same thing.)

No sabe ni lo que suena atrás.
> He doen't even know what is making noise behind him. (He's oblivious to what is going on.)

No tiene crianza, ni moralidad, ni pelo en la lengua.
> She doesn't have respect, morality, nor hair on her tongue. (Said of a disrespectful, immoral, and vile-speaking person.)

No vale ni un cero a la izquierda.
> He's not worth even a zero to the left side.

Víctor Serrano, Rincón de los Trujillos, 2010.

A Pachanga in Rincón de los Trujillos

Si un pobre se emborracha es tontería; si un rico se emborracha es alegría.
If a poor man gets drunk, it is foolishness; if a rich man gets drunk, it is merriment.

A friend of mine, Sam Adams, joins me for a jaunt to Chimayó today. I rarely bring "outsiders" with me on my Chimayó trips, but Sam, with his unassuming manner and candid, open respect for everyone he meets, has a way of fitting in anywhere.

I wanted Sam to meet Esequiel, and we're disappointed to find he isn't home. We pass his house and barns beside the badlands on the north side of the Santa Cruz Valley. The sight of Alonzo's two horses, pacing the rickety old corrals, compels me to pull over and take some photographs. I'm clicking away in the noonday sun when a small car trailing a cloud of dust comes down the road and slows near me. I tense, expecting a scolding or an admonition to get out of the road and away from this place, where tourists—and I look like one with my camera—are not often seen. Adopting a cheerful expression, I walk over to the stopped car. The window opens, and a sixtyish woman smoking a cigarette leans across the seat to greet me.

"Isn't this beautiful?" she asks. I agree it is.

"I love it here," she goes on. "I drive past here every day, just to see this part of Chimayó. I never get tired of it."

"Me, too," I say. "That's why I love to take pictures out here."

"Oh, yes," she says, making a sweeping motion with her hand to take in the view of the Sangre de Cristo Mountains, framed by bone-dry badland cliff faces. "You've got to enjoy these back roads because this is the real America. This is America the beautiful! I lived in Santa Fe for a while, but my biggest mistake was in not staying here. I had to come back to Chimayó."

"Oh, so you're from here?" I ask.

"Actually, I'm a Vigil from Cundiyó, from the Vigils up there, but the Vigils and the Trujillos and Ortegas from Chimayó are all related," she goes on. "I'm Roberta. My sister and I live here in Chimayó now, just down the road there."

"And why do you like to drive this back road?"

"For the beauty of it!" Roberta exclaims. "Oh my God, it's like as if I'm in heaven. If I die tomorrow, I can say I've been in heaven on these back roads. Ain't that the truth?"

"Amen, sister!" I respond. "The Vigils from Cundiyó? I have relatives there."

"Really? Who?"

"Well, let's see. My great-great-aunt Gelacia Ortega Chávez married Longino Vigil from Cundiyó. She and Longino were the parents of Noberto, Pulas, Marcos, and all those Vigils."

"Oh, sí! My Tío Marcos," she replies. "I grew up with him. He was one of the first weavers in Cundiyó. And Esquipulas was my grandpa José Dolores's brother. I put together all those names by looking at the Cundiyó land grant papers. I got the land grant and put together who was the brother of who."

"We used to visit primo Noberto at his store there in Cundiyó," I tell her.

"Oh, I used to work in that little store when I was a little girl!" she squeals with delight. "I got paid a penny, and I was so happy! I knew every single house in Cundiyó, and I still go up and visit."

Roberta tells me she has to be on her way to a graduation party for a relative on "that side of the family," and she's off. I return to my truck, where Sam is waiting.

"You know, as soon as you start talking to people here in Chimayó, your accent changes, and you speak like them," he comments. "You pronounce all your words differently."

I hadn't noticed, but apparently Sam sees me slip into a Chimayó persona while I'm here.

I take Sam on a spin through Chimayó, pointing out the various plazas. Near Rincón we pass a group of motorcyclists gathered in the dirt parking area in front of a house. Sam and I both glance at them, and I remark, "It would be great to take photographs there, but . . ."

"Well, let's go," Sam says. "What could happen? All they could do is to tell us to leave."

I can think of all kinds of things that might happen, but this attitude is why Sam gets such great photographs. He's fearless and forthright and charming, and he's made photographs of people the world over. His engaging personality, as well as a discerning eye and razor-sharp intellect, was also the key to his successful career as a Hollywood agent. I turn into the yard and stop in the middle of the assembled Harleys.

A young man strides toward my truck immediately. *"Me siento como cabra en corral ajeno.*—I feel like a goat in someone else's corral," I think to myself, and my trepidation increases when the biker barks out at me, "What the f—— you doing here!"

"I'm taking pictures around Chimayó and thought it would be cool to get some of you guys."

"What?" he says. "Pictures for what?"

"For a book, I hope," I reply.

He scowls at me, and another twenty-something dude, in a black leather vest, strides over. He's plastered with finely crafted tattoos.

"What's happening?" he asks.

"He says he wants to take pictures of us!" the first guy states, with an expression of incredulity.

"Well, that's cool," says the second, turning to me. "I love artists, and obviously you're an artist"—gesturing to my camera—"so that's why I say, go for it, do whatever you want to do. I'm an artist, too."

"What kind of artist are you?" I ask.

"I'm a tattoo artist," he replies, pointing to the elaborate reticulation of dark blue lines on his forearm, "but I do a lot of contemporary art, too."

Then the door to the house beside the yard opens and out strides Roberta, whom I had just met down the road.

"Hey, I know you!" she says. And then, to the gathering knot of bikers, "He's from around here. His *parientes* are from the plaza."

At that, the guard goes down. The artist biker puts out his hand.

"Víctor Serrano," he says. "From Española."

Others in the group follow suit, and soon I'm milling among them, chatting and making pictures of them and their bikes. Roberta's niece Dolores Lucero and her partner, Vince Apodaca, introduce themselves before firing up their bike and roaring off down the road. A young woman leaning back on a parked bike and smoking a cigarette catches my eye. She wears a black bandanna, jeans rolled up to show her calves, a Red River 2010 T-shirt, and shiny black high-heeled sandals. A portrait of a suffering Jesus crowned with thorns adorns the bright blue gas tank of the bike. Hands folded in prayer are airbrushed on the front fender. The woman's boyfriend comes up from behind, grabs her tightly, and kisses her repeatedly. Roberta walks over and hugs the couple, then introduces me to her daughter, Odessa Chávez.

I ask how Roberta came up with the name Odessa for her daughter.

"Oh, it's a long story," she says. "I had lost a daughter in an accident a few months before Odessa was born. So when I was gonna have her I went to the hospital because it was an emergency. I was in labor, and she was coming fast, and I got to the emergency room, but they were so busy that my niece ended up delivering the baby. There were no doctors around! So my niece said, 'What are you going to name her?' And I couldn't even think, and someone—my niece or the nurse—just said, 'We'll call her Odessa.'"

Sam gets out of the truck and strolls over to the crowd. He's received with friendly curiosity. I introduce him as my photographer friend. Víctor steps out first to shake his hand and says, "Sam Adams? I know your work, man!"

Sam and I look at each other skeptically. "Sam Adams" is a name familiar to everyone, more because of the beer by that name than because of any memory of the historical American patriot. But Sam humors Víctor. "Oh yeah, my photographs are all over the place—it was probably at the Museum of Modern Art."

"No, for reals," Víctor says. "It was in Madrid, down by Cerrillos, about two years ago. I ride there a lot to check out galleries, especially photography. I saw your work there. I love black-and-white pictures. I liked that one you had there of some tango dancers."

Sam looks at me, astonished. It seems incredible that Víctor could know Sam's photographs, but he is right on with every point. Sam had just such a show in Madrid. The connection further relaxes everyone.

There's some commotion over by the house as another biker, this one shaved bald and wearing a white muscle shirt, emerges from the door, whooping and holding out his arm. A crowd forms around him as he shows off a tattoo, freshly drawn. There's still blood on the fine blue lines of a sunglass-bearing skull surrounded by flames, stretched to cover all of his forearm. The man proudly holds out his arm for me to photograph and introduces himself as Sam Vigil. Then he turns his back to me to show me another, older tattoo on the back of his arm: CHIMA spelled out in stylized lettering.

Following Sam Vigil out the door comes the tattooist who just adorned his arm, Aniceto Chávez, shirtless, barefoot, tattooed (of course), and followed by his nine-year-old mini-me-like son, also named Aniceto. Like everyone else in this bunch, Aniceto senior (whom they call Cheto) carries a Bud and offers me one. I accept. I haven't had a Bud since high school.

"So you're a Chávez?" I ask.

"Yes. ¿Conoce a los Chávez?—You know the Chávezes?" he asks.

"*Mi mamá es Chávez, de allá de Potrero.*—My mother is Chávez, from over there in Potrero," I tell him.

"I come from Mexico, from Chihuahua," he says, with a tone that seems half-apologetic, lapsing into perfect English.

"We're related to those Chávezes, too," I say. "One of my great-great-grandfathers went back to Mexico during the Pueblo Revolt, and he came back here, but some of his relatives stayed behind in Chihuahua."

"No way!" Roberta chimes up from behind me, and she interjects that she, too, has relatives in the Chávez family. But before we can explore that connection, Cheto leads me inside the house to show me his tattooing setup.

He works in a cluttered back bedroom. A giant portrait of Hernán Cortez hangs on the wall above his work space, a small cleared spot on a desk. Cheto explains that he paints and draws, too, and holds up a framed pencil drawing of the Last Supper, intricately rendered. Almost all his work bears religious symbology or Aztecan figures and glyphs. He brims with enthusiasm for his art. People come from all around for his tattoos, he says.

Back outside, a car pulls into the driveway in a big hurry and skids to a stop. I go out to see about the commotion. A young man, shirtless and tattooed, jumps out and says to me, "What the hell is going on here?"

"A party, I guess," I answer.

"Party? Well this is my mom's house, and we don't know about any f——ing party. She's pissed, and I'm here to kick some ass because she told me to!"

Some of the bikers approach him and a heated discussion begins, then his mother gets down from the car and walks over. For some reason she, too, asks me what is going on, as if I'm in charge. I explain I'm just here taking pictures. But it turns out she is the stepdaughter of a friend of mine in Los Ranchos, down by the Santa Cruz River. She introduces herself as Loretta. She asks who started the party, and I again profess ignorance. But within a few minutes, after fresh beers are distributed, all is well. The party resumes. When Loretta sees I'm taking pictures, she turns around and pulls up her shirt to show me the tattoos on her back: rotund, multicolored dragons breathing smoke and flames while floating amid planets and stars.

Dragon symbols have long been linked with the use of heroin and other opiates. "Chasing the dragon" is a metaphor for the quest for the ultimate high. Some say the dragon outright symbolizes *chiva*, or heroin, in northern New Mexico. But Loretta's whimsical dragons seem playful and not in the least bit sinister. In fact, Loretta works with a local nonprofit organization to help people avoid or kick addictions of all kinds. Like so much else about Chimayó, the danger perceived in outward appearances is usually only skin-deep.

DICHOS ABOUT CHARACTER

Nomás los muertos no hacen ruido.
> Only dead people don't make noise. (A response from somebody who is criticized for talking too much.)

Pide limosna para hacer caridades.
> She asks for alms so she can give to charity. (She asks for gifts so she can turn around and do charitable deeds to make herself important.)

Piedra movediza nunca moja la cobija.
> A rolling stone gathers no moss. (Said of a person who hasn't settled down yet.)

Piensa que nomás su silla no mata.
> He thinks his saddle is the only one that doesn't cause sores. (Said of someone who thinks he does no wrong.)

Piensa que nomás sus naranjas valen.
> She thinks only her oranges are worth something. (Refers to a person who thinks she is above everybody else.)

¿Qué importa jamones y leche nevada si los corazones no ambicionan nada?
> What does it matter if you have ham and ice cream if you do not have ambition? (Wealth without ambition is empty.)

Quien calla, otorga.
> He who is silent gives consent. (If you don't agree, speak up.)

Quiere pasar la acequia antes de llegar a la puente.
>She wants to cross the ditch before she gets to the bridge. (Said of someone who wants to advance without starting at the beginning.)

Quiere saber del huevo y quién lo puso.
>He wants to know about the egg and who laid it. (Said of a nosy person.)

Represente quince por docena.
>She represents fifteen for a dozen. (Said of a person who brags she has more than she really has.)

Se apuran más los ordeñadores que los dueños del ganado.
>The milkers hurry more than the owners of the herd. (Said of a worker who concerns himself more about a business than the owners themselves do.)

Se está curando en salud.
>She is healing herself despite being healthy. (She is defending herself before being accused of anything.)

Esequiel Trujillo, Los Ojuelos, 2009.

Adiós Andariego

Las enfermedades entran corriendo y salen despacio.
Illnesses strike suddenly and leave slowly.

It's a dry June day, and I drive straight to Esequiel's. It concerned me greatly when he wasn't home last time I visited. Soon I'll be leaving for a couple of weeks, so I want to check in with him as well as his daughter, Loyola, and her husband, Ralph.

Loyola, sitting on the low wall around the front porch having a smoke, informs me Esequiel is asleep, and of course we don't want to disturb him. She looks exhausted, as does Ralph when he comes out to join her. Their two rowdy grandsons follow him into the warm late afternoon air.

I inquire about Esequiel's health, and I'm stunned by the news. When I had asked Esequiel about his visits to the doctor over the past months, he said he had "*una bola de sangre*—a ball of blood" in his abdomen, and that it had been removed. I asked if it was cancer, and he didn't reply but expressed confidence the problem was taken care of. Even as I watched him losing weight and growing weaker, I was convinced he would recover.

But now I learn what he meant by "una bola de sangre." Loyola says Esequiel was visiting doctors in Santa Fe last week, to follow up on the operation he had last fall, when they removed a tumor. He's just been in for a checkup, and the prognosis is not good. A new mass has been growing quickly. They don't think he has much time.

The dreaded sentence "We gave him his pills and he's resting quietly" floats in the suddenly dense air.

Looking around the property I've become very familiar with, I decide to go for a walk as a way to take in this news by myself. The heavy sadness around the house feels oppressive. I wander away from Esequiel's to explore a little, heading over to a nearby house belonging to Esequiel's cousin, Narciso. The place has intrigued me for years.

Near Narciso's house I pause at a cushioned chair sitting in the shade of a raggedy Siberian elm. Getting closer, I see there are actually two chairs jammed together, one a beat-up wood-frame chair covered with a piece of corrugated roofing, the other a worn La-Z-Boy, light tan in color, with a mismatched blue cushion. Beside them leans a weathered gray table of rough lumber hastily nailed together. I remember seeing Narciso sitting here on summer evenings like this one, looking out over the empty fields that, in his youth, were covered with crops. Now that he's moved away, there's no one to sit in the chairs. Everyone is too busy.

Thick smoke from a fire somewhere to the west has turned the light a deep wine-red color. Near the chairs, also apart from the house, Narciso's rickety *gallinero* (chicken coop) is turning crimson in the evening sun. The coop presents a study in entropy valiantly resisted: an assortment of boards of a hundred dimensions, strands of rusted barbed wire, and sheets of corrugated metal in various stages of weathering away.

A makeshift security fence made of another random collection of boards of various sizes encircles the house. Many of the vertical boards are split or cut to make sharp points, forming a stockade-like barrier. I peer beyond this to see inside the small patio surrounding the house: more easy chairs here and there, all in a ragged condition but still somehow inviting and suggestive of comfort. One in particular, perched near the main entrance to the house, seems about to melt into the swirl of leaves at its base. Stuffing hangs from its innards, and the cushions from a much smaller but slightly less worn chair have been placed atop it as a hasty repair. Near an outbuilding, yet another easy chair leans, this one covered with a scrap of floor carpeting and flanked by a small doghouse.

Some of the adobe walls of the house and outbuilding have been plastered with stucco. Others have been covered with chicken wire lathe, but never plastered. Still others show the raw mud, cracked and crumbling, of the original construction. The whole place is a monument to ingenuity on a Chimayó budget.

The sun touches the rim of the Valles Caldera to the west as I return to

Esequiel's house. He's fully awake as I sit down at his bedside. Although his voice is a bit hoarse, he asks about my family. When I inquire about his health, he says he's getting better. When I tell him I'll be gone for a couple of weeks, he says, "*O, qué bueno. Que Dios le bendiga en su camino.*—Oh, how nice. May God bless you on your way." He reaches out for me, and for a moment it seems he's going to give me the *bendición*, the blessing, an old tradition my grandmother used to practice.

I'm transported back to a time when I was leaving Chimayó for a month-long trip. Grandma was 101 years old and was lying in bed when my wife, Deborah, and I came to say good-bye. At first Grandma expressed her extreme displeasure at our impending departure, giving us a good scolding.

"*¡Andariegos! ¿Qué buscan allá tan lejos? ¡Andan buscando peligro, es lo que hacen! ¡Andan con las colas paradas!*—You wanderers, you! What are you looking for over there so far away? You're looking for danger, that's what you're doing! You run around with your tails up in the air!"

She went on to characterize me as even worse than an andariego: a *vagabundo*, a vagrant or a bum, which was quite a derogatory term in the conservative, place-bound culture she came from. To her generation of Chimayosos, anyone who wasn't rooted in place was highly suspect. In fact, the word *vagabundo* turns up describing the worst kind of criminals in one old document in our collection, wherein José Antonio and José Guadalupe López accuse one of the Olivas brothers of being a "*vagabundo.*" Juan Cristóbal Archuleta, who tried to break things up, goes even farther, calling the López brothers "*vagabundos provocativos,*" quarrelsome bums.

Once her outburst subsided, Grandma asked us to kneel beside her bed so she could reach us. Then, one at a time, she blessed us in the old way, making the sign of the cross on our foreheads while saying, "*La bendición de Dios Padre, Dios Hijo, Dios Espíritu Santo y después la mía te alcance.*—The blessing of God the Father, the Son, the Holy Spirit, and then mine, that it may reach you."

It was a solemn and sincere send-off, and I feel the same spirit now as Esequiel reaches toward me. I never knew my grandfathers—both died in their forties—but I'm swept away with the thought that my grandfather Abedón would have spoken to me just like this. I imagine Abedón giving me the blessing as Esequiel touches my head and grasps my hand, repeating, "*Que Dios le bendiga en su camino.*" And I imagine another voice muttering, "Vagabundo!"

Matachín traje in Esequiel Trujillo's house, 2010.

DICHOS ABOUT CHARACTER

Se estira una oreja y no se alcanza la otra.
    He pulls one ear and can't reach the other one. (Said when a person has done something foolish and it's too late do anything about it.)

Se le olvidó el nombre del chaquegüe pero del meneadillo, no.
    She forgot the word for cornmeal mush but not how to stir it. (Said of a someone who has forgotten her roots.)

Se ofrece largo y queda corto.
    He generously offers to help and then backs out. (It is easier to make promises than to keep them.)

Se quedó amolada y sin cortar.
    She was left sharpened but did not get to cut. (Said when a woman is stood up.)

Se quedó para vestir santos.
    She was left to dress the saints. (Said when a woman didn't get married and now spends her time attending to the statues in the church.)

Si no es santo es porque no lo cuelgan.
    If he's not a saint, it's only because they don't hang him on the wall. (Good deeds and selflessness often go unrecognized.)

Si un pobre se emborracha es tontería; si un rico se emborracha es alegría.
    If a poor man gets drunk, it is foolishness; if a rich man gets drunk, it is merriment. (Poverty is considered a vice by those who are not poor.)

Sí, ya se sabe de qué pie cojea.
    Yes, we all know on which foot he limps. (He can't fool anybody.)

Esequiel Trujillo's truck, 2010.

Esequiel Takes a Spin

Nadie se lleva lo que tiene.
Nobody takes with him what he owns.

Traveling on my own today, I drive directly to Esequiel's. Since I've returned from my travels, I've heard he's doing poorly, and I want to see firsthand what that means.

It's a blazing-hot day. Cicadas buzz in the piñón trees along the dusty road. The horses in Esequiel's corrals doze in the midday sun, crowding in the shade of a juniper, head to tail. I arrive at Esequiel's house and hurry to the door, carrying with me a case of bottled water for him (he will only drink bottled water now) and a case of Bud Light for Ralph and Loyola, who I know are worn and worried from caring for Esequiel.

I tiptoe into the kitchen and set down my cargo, noticing candles burning on the table beside everyday kitchen-table items. Above the table hangs a porcelain portrait of Jesus and a framed print of a duck in flight. Another candle flickers in Esequiel's room, next to a bottle of aspirin and prescription drugs on his dresser. The candles impress me as ominous portents. Through the doorway to the living room, I see Ralph sleeping soundly on the couch. The television drones, an inane game show.

Loyola is bent over Eseqiel in his room. His skeletal figure rises like a feather in her hands as she lifts and turns him. He lets out a groan, and his head rolls toward me. I wave weakly, stunned at the decline in his health. He seems not to see me when I enter the room. Loyola asks if I can stay with him for a while and takes her leave for a much-needed break. I sit by the bed and hold Esequiel's hand.

"*Gracias por venir.*—Thanks for coming," he says, recognizing me and tightly gripping my hand. His voice comes out in a whisper. I notice a small plastic bag pinned to his pajama top, inside it a tiny, twisted root. I ask what it is. "*Oshá*," Esequiel mumbles, referring to the wild celery plant long used in New Mexico for curing all kinds of illness. "*Me ayuda.*—It helps me."

After long moments of silence, Esequiel begins talking. I can barely hear or understand him. He talks and talks, hoarsely, asking for water now and then, his voice reminding me all too clearly of the squeaky tones of my grandma's voice when she braved out her final days. Esequiel rambles on about his life, a nonstop monologue that barely rises in volume above the sound of the TV in the other room.

The host of the game show says, "For one thousand dollars, the final question: What is an arroyo?"

Esequiel chatters on: "*Trabajaba hasta las seis de la mañana y luego llegué a la casa para ayudar a los niños en preparar para la escuela, pero dijo mi papá, '¿Por qué apuras tanto a regresar cada mañana? Yo puedo cuidar a los niños bien.' Pero yo quería regresar a ver a mis hijos . . .*—I worked until six in the morning and then arrived home to help the kids get ready for school, but my father said to me, 'Why do you rush home every morning? I can take care of the kids just fine.' But I wanted to come back to see my kids . . ."

Esequiel goes on to tell a story about a horseback ride he took as a kid, up into the barrancas on the north side of the valley, when somehow he lost his horse and had to walk a very long distance to get home. Then he's on to another memory of his father and another childhood adventure. I sit and nod and squeeze Esequiel's hand. Finally he dozes off. The house is quiet, save for the ongoing jabber from the TV that sits above the drum-turned-coffee-table made from a cottonwood log. I wander around the house. Now both Ralph and Loyola are asleep in the living room. On the wall above Loyola hangs a portrait of her long-dead mother and a Matachín palma, while above Ralph there are a Matachín corona and an array of cloth dolls representing the various Matachines characters.

A fan whirs, but the heat is oppressive. I sit at the kitchen table for a while, then walk out and around the house and nearby property, taking pictures of a '55 Chevy Impala, a Cadillac from the '60s, Loyola's '75 Cougar (which Esequiel bought for her when she was graduating from high school), the Oldsmobile, the crumbling shed, a set of battered folding chairs—and checking back now and then to see if anyone is awake.

I'm behind the ramshackle structure that serves as a home for Esequiel's son

Lorenzo when I'm startled by a loud shout: "¡*Qué anda haciendo aquí, cabrón! ¡Vete, vete! ¡Quítate de aquí!*—What are you doing around here, f——er! Go on, go on! Get out of here!" I jump from looking through my tripod-mounted camera to find Lorenzo behind me, approaching rapidly and aggressively. The thoughts flash through my mind, "*Ya me anda la lumbre a los aparejos*—The fire is up to my pack saddles" (meaning trouble is just about to catch up with me) and "*Aquí me metí en camisa de once varas*—I got myself in a shirt eleven varas long" (or, I got myself into trouble I don't know how to get out of).

I realize that Lorenzo doesn't know who I am, and I call out, "Lorenzo! It's me!" It takes a few repetitions before he hears me and stops in his tracks, but his anger is not assuaged.

"You know, man, you're welcome around here, because we know your *gente* and my dad likes you and all that, but you just can't go sneaking around, especially back here. See that house on the hill? Those people there, they'll *kill* you if they see you out there. You never know what could happen. It's like *Alice in Wonderland*, man, the things that can happen. You're walking along and all of a sudden, things can get real weird, real heavy."

"*Ya más claro no canta el gallo.*—The rooster can't crow any more clearly," I say to myself. It's obvious I shouldn't snoop around here.

I apologize and promise not to wander back there anymore—and Lorenzo offers me a beer and invites me in his house. It's another Bud, but at least it's not a Light. We duck low through the doorway into his humble abode, a remodeled outbuilding recently fitted with plumbing and electricity. The roof is made of layers of corrugated metal. Lorenzo, wearing *pecheras* (overalls) with no shirt underneath, is still visibly shaken from the start I gave him. He gradually calms down as he shows me around the two rooms, but we can't stay inside long. The heat is too much, and we exit to sit in the shade outside. Eventually, Loyola comes out of Esequiel's house, rubbing her eyes. It's early evening.

"We're gonna get Dad ready and see if we can take him out for a ride," she says, pointing to the electrically powered wheelchair parked in the kitchen. Ralph stirs, and together he and Loyola dress Esequiel in a warm flannel shirt, sweatpants, socks, and slippers. Esequiel grabs from the table a flat cap like one a golfer would wear and sets it awkwardly on his head; it must be a gift from the hospice nurses who visit him. I'm struck by the contrast of his attire now, hanging on his shriveled frame, with the jeans, boots, black cowboy hat, and work jacket he wore when first I met him. That outfit, and his proud, erect stance, once so defined his character. I hear in my mind the dicho grandma used for a man showing his age: "*Ya la espiga va para abajo.*—The spike of wheat is starting to bend down."

Loyola and Ralph lift Esequiel and place him gently in the chair. He lets out a groan but settles in. The small kitchen proves a difficult space for maneuvering the four-wheeled device. Ralph tells me how he and Loyola found this out yesterday, when Ralph leaned over Esequiel and pushed the lever to engage the motor and drive the chair forward. The small nudge he gave the control was just a little too much. The chair took off and in a split second rocketed across the kitchen and slammed into the door jam. As Ralph tells it, Esequiel bounced like a rag doll but somehow stayed in the chair. Ralph, Loyola, and I double over with laughter as Ralph recounts the incident. Esequiel manages a wan smile.

We're able to just barely squeeze the chair through the door and out into the yard. The device moves easily, tank-like, over the uneven dirt of the yard and out the farm gate. Loyola asks which way Esequiel wants to go, and he gestures to the north, up the long driveway. He takes control of the chair, manipulating the little joystick with one hand, and bumps along in the cooling evening air, glancing this way and that at a place he's known all his life. It's a stark contrast to see him driving the little motorized chair past his old truck, a massive and powerful machine he once commanded. The heavy adobes he stacked there, the heavy cottonwood rounds he cut and manhandled into the cab, the farm gate he hung—all these things bear testament to Esequiel's former strength and energy, now drained.

Esequiel stops in front of Don Benigno's house.

"*¿Allí nació, no?*—You were born there, right?" I ask.

He nods and gazes at the house for a moment, then turns back down the driveway toward his own home, his garrulous manner stilled.

On the way back, a whimpering and whining sound draws our attention. I investigate and discover a litter of eight pit bull puppies beneath a defunct Chevy Impala in a thicket beside the driveway. I'm bending low to lure them out when a gruff voice barks out, "Hey! You gonna pay me for taking pictures of my dogs?!"

I jump around to find myself face to face with a stout, clean-shaven man in a ragged, stained T-shirt, his baseball hat on backward and a cigarette hanging from his lips. I grin and come out with, "If I make any money, maybe." And then, pointing toward the puppies: "Where's the mama?"

"She's around here somewhere," he says, extending his hand and letting out a friendly laugh.

"I'm Alonzo. Esequiel's son. But don't take my picture! I just came from work."

I introduce myself, and we chat about the dogs—he plans to sell the puppies—as we proceed back down the driveway in procession, Esequiel leading silently in his chair. Sadly, the sight brings to mind a dicho, "*Ya no dura los truenos de mayo.*—He won't last through May's thunder," meaning he won't last long.

Back at home, Esequiel returns to bed, and the vigil resumes. A van pulls up, and two women emerge, Liliana and Lurdie, cousins of Esequiel's. They've come to take a shift at sitting with him. Alonzo heads home, while Ralph and Loyola take a short break to check on their house next door. Liliana and Lurdie and I sit under the portal in the warm twilight and visit.

Lurdie's name is a shortening of Librada. I tell her my great-great-aunt was named Librada, but people called her Libradita or Mama Lita. "Who was your aunt?" she asks, and we're off on the conversation about who is related to whom. It's a long talk that leads down many pathways. Our pedigrees don't intersect, but we do discover I knew Liliana's deceased husband, Cecilio, who used to sell produce at the Farmers Market in Española. I have a photo of him I promise to bring her someday.

I pull out a box of the pictures I've been taking, and they're amused to see so many Chimayosos they know. Lurdie identifies one of the men at the biker party as Sam Vigil, although she calls him Samito. I've been trying to locate Sam so I can give him a picture, but I haven't found his house. She offers to take it to him. Then I ask if I can take their photos to add to the collection, and they laugh loudly but don't protest when I begin shooting in the near darkness. Every once in a while, one of the women goes inside to check on Esequiel. He's sleeping deeply. When I look at the array of prescription bottles on the kitchen table and reflect on Esequiel's wracked body, I can't help but think, "*Es peor el remedio que la enfermedad.*—The remedy is worse than the illness." Esequiel is too weak to open his eyes or talk, and I don't even try to address him.

In a while, Ralph returns and hands me a beer, and Loyola joins us. Ralph sits on a low bench under the portal. The glow from their cigarettes sparks light in the gloom. It's going to be a long night. It's a good thing I brought a full case of beer.

Esequiel Takes a Spin

DICHOS ABOUT CHARACTER

Son de la misma caballada.
>They are from the same herd of horses. (They are of the same clique or political party.)

Son pájaros de la misma pluma.
>They are birds of a feather. (Said of two people who are similar in all aspects.)

Tanto va el cántaro al agua hasta que se rompe.
>The pitcher makes so many trips to get water, it finally breaks. (Said when a person plays too much with fire and finally gets burned.)

Tiene más entradas que salidas.
>He has more entries than exits. (Said of someone who thinks he is very smart, but isn't.)

Tanto peca él que agarra la pata como él que mata la vaca.
>He who takes the leg sins as much as he who kills the cow. (The accomplice to a crime is just as guilty as the criminal, no matter how small a part he plays.)

Un árbol que crece torcido nunca su rama endereza.
>A tree that grows up crooked never straightens its branches. (Early mistakes are not easily corrected.)

Viejo retobado, muchacho malcriado.
> Mean old man, disrespectful boy. (Character is determined at an early age.)

Ya no suena ni truena.
> He no longer makes noise or thunder. (He is old and feeble, or he is no longer popular.)

Salomón Trujillo and his Chihuahua, Los Ojuelos, 2010.

Salomón

A tu tierra, grulla, que esta no es tuya.
Go back to your home, crane, for this land isn't yours.

I'm still a bit shaken up by my encounter with Lorenzo and haunted by the thought that I could have been in serious trouble with that neighbor on the hill. I imagine him up there with a rifle, watching for me to come around again. So, on my way to check on Esequiel again, I stop at the home of a neighbor of his, Diane, on the pretense of photographing a moldering 1957 Chevy in back of her house. Really I want to ask about the mysterious and dangerous man on the hill.

Diane breaks into a hearty laugh when I tell her the story. "He's not dangerous," she chuckles. "His name is Salomón, and you can go see for yourself. Tell him I sent you."

So I drive around behind Diane's house and approach the place on the hill, a handcrafted building obviously constructed in phases. With trepidation, I open the gate to the small yard and immediately hear a dog yapping furiously. I let out a shouted hello and hear stirring inside. In a few minutes, a figure makes its way to the door and an old man opens it, greeting me with a puzzled smile as he scoops up the Chihuahua at his feet.

Salomón's face radiates humor and openness, and all my trepidation vanishes. After all, "*El bien y el mal a la cara sale.*—Good and evil are reflected in the face," and this is clearly an expression of kindness.

Salomón invites me into his kitchen, welcomes the dog on to his lap, and asks why I've come to visit him. I skip the story about him being a scary fellow and tell him about my quest to explore Chimayó and meet people. He's amused, engaged, and willing to tell me his story. But first he puts on some water for coffee.

The violence I'd so feared could erupt seems a ludicrous, paranoid fantasy now. Yet I know just how real such scenarios are in Chimayó and how quickly I can become ensnared in them—even acting out the violence myself. I shudder to remember when I was a hairsbreadth from pulling a trigger.

Soon after the plaza bully had killed my dog and threatened me, my father came to Chimayó with a small pistol. He called it a "man stopper" and implored me to carry it with me, at least for a while. He feared that the next time I was assaulted I would not come out unscathed. After much discussion I agreed to carry the gun for a month or two.

Just weeks later, I was taking a walk into the hills, and there he was, my antagonist, waiting for me. He jumped from behind a juniper and shouted at me. There was a fence between us, and he stopped there, cursing at me and beckoning me toward him. I lifted the gun in my pocket, leveled it at him, and placed my finger on the trigger, keeping the weapon hidden. It was a .38 caliber snub-nosed revolver, five shot. The lead-tipped bullet was designed to enter a body and spread wide, carving out a huge, bleeding wound. It was meant to stop an attacker dead at close range, my father had explained. I imagined just such a scenario and envisioned myself dragging this 250-pound corpse back to my house across the road, as the policeman had supposedly coached my neighbor to do.

He lifted his foot and placed in on a strand of barbed wire as if to jump over. I thought of the irony that this fence line marked the boundary of property first claimed by my ancestors in the early 1700s, the boundary marked by the blue rock on the hillside. The family papers record a dispute about this property soon after it was claimed. Now, over two hundred years later, another disagreement has brought neighbors to conflict along the same line.

If he crosses that fence, I thought, I'll shoot. My finger tightened on the trigger, and I pointed toward his sagging gut. But he didn't climb over.

I turned my back on him, the hair raised on my neck, and listened for the fall of his footsteps if he should jump the fence and chase me. He didn't. When I returned home, I emptied all the rounds from the revolver and locked it in an outbuilding. I never held it again, and I gave it away after my father died some time later.

As Salomón and I sip coffee and he tells me of his life, I reflect on how close I came to participating in the violence that so often flares in this valley that I love, feeling grateful that my fears proved unfounded this time.

And yet I know that Lorenzo's outburst, while misidentifying Salomón as a danger to me, is fair assessment of a sentiment among many here. The antagonism toward strangers nosing around can be very real.

DICHOS ABOUT HEALTH

Entre verde y seco, pero mas seco que verde.
    Between verdant and dried up, but more dry than green. (Said when one is not feeling too well).

Es peor el remedio que la enfermedad.
    The remedy is worse than the illness.

Las enfermedades entran corriendo y salen despacio.
    Illnesses strike quickly and leave slowly.

Más viejo es el aire y todavía sopla.
    Much older is the wind, and it still blows. (Said of older people still full of life.)

No hay mal que dure cien años ni enfermo que los aguante.
    There is no sickness that lasts a hundred years nor a sick person who can endure so long. (Someone can't stay mad at you forever.)

Soy como el cerco de rama: no sirve pero algo ayuda.
    I am like fence made from branches, which doesn't work very well but helps somewhat. (Said of an old person who can't do much anymore.)

Tras de ser malo, es caro.
    In addition to being bad for you, it's expensive. (Said of a costly bad habit.)

Patricio Cruz's abandoned house near Los Ranchos, 2010.

Don Patricio Cruz's House on the Hill

Ya está viejo Pedro para cabrero.
Pedro is too old to be a goatherder.

This balmy November afternoon I vow to get a close look at a lone adobe house sitting on a hilltop smack in the middle of the valley. It's a house that draws attention and invites stories: it's old, crumbling, isolated, and visible from many vantages. It's situated in the middle of a large, undeveloped pasture, one of a dwindling number left in Chimayó.

This was the home of Don Patricio Cruz not many years ago. When I was growing up, it seemed everyone in Chimayó knew Don Patricio, but he didn't earn his renown by being particularly flamboyant or notorious in any way. Instead, he had a high profile because he herded goats, lots of goats, and he sold milk to many families around the Plaza del Cerro—and he did so for a very long time. My grandmother and her peers remembered getting milk from him when they were young, and they described in nostalgic terms Don Patricio's daily ritual of driving the goats up to the hills and back down to the valley. His passage through the neighborhood was a comforting marker of time and a reminder of the slower pace of days gone by.

Since I've been exploring Chimayó anew, as an adult, the structure has beckoned. And today I stop in at a neighbor's place, whose owners I know well. Chris and Nancy bought the house, a beautiful adobe that once belonged to Anselmo Ortiz. I reason they must know whom I can contact to get to the dilapidated structure on the hill.

Chris and Nancy welcome me and show me around their comfortable home. Across a field stands an abandoned house, an ancient barn made of logs, and a row of defunct automobiles, all of them mellowing slowly and melting away. Chris and Nancy aren't sure who owns the Cruz house a quarter mile away, but when they turn me loose to wander around their property, I'm inexorably drawn to the buildings and cars. They are transforming under the hand of time, their colors fading, their forms sagging gracefully.

I'm deep in the thrall of photographing the late afternoon light on a rusted Oldsmobile when I hear footsteps and the rattle of a dog's collar. I turn to see a man and a large black dog crossing the fields toward Don Patricio's house. Realizing it's another Patricio—Pat Martínez, an old friend from my days on the board of directors of the Chimayó Mutual Domestic Water Association—I call out. Pat returns the greeting and walks over to the fence line separating us, where we meet and shake hands.

Pat is a distant cousin to me, through an unusual link. His mother was Sofía Maestas, and her grandmother Francisca was a *criada*, or household servant, in my great-great-great-grandfather Francisco Antonio Mestas's home in La Puebla. (The Mestas family name was later changed to Maestas.) Francisco (a.k.a. El Güero Mestas) fathered children by both his legal wife and Francisca. Both lineages proudly claim him as their progenitor, and El Güero included Francisca in his will along with his wife. You might say Pat is my distant half cousin, but the relationship doesn't come up in our conversation today.

Pat was a steady presence on the water board. He kept a clear head when the water system broke down (which it did frequently) and residents began quarreling over who should fix it and how. Pat was willing to lend a hand and pick up a shovel. I knew he owned land and kept cows down in the lowlands by the river, and I'm delighted to know he's on his way out to check on the livestock, who roam not only his property but also, with the permission of the current owners, the property where Don Patricio's house stands. I tell him of my obsession about seeing Don Patricio's humble abode, and he suggests I follow him out on his daily chore.

So finally, after years of gazing out at the place, I'm walking up toward that storied building, and as the distance between me and the house closes, I find it ever more compelling. It's another Chimayó time capsule, sitting for decades, untouched. Beside it, the roof of Don Patricio's old barn lies intact on top of its walls, canted at a crazy angle. When I last studied the buildings from a distance, just a few years ago, the barn was standing. Ruins of other adobe outbuildings tumble nearby.

The west-facing door to Don Patricio's two-story home is held shut with a single fence post and a piece of bailing wire; the door on the opposite wall is similarly wired to a screen door laid horizontally on its side. I peer in through broken windows. Some of Don Patricio's furniture is still there, tables and chairs lying in disarray, thick with dust. Coffee cans and a few plastic dishes litter the floor, and through an open closet door, I can see rows of moth-eaten shirts and jackets hanging. Pat explains that Don Patricio's nephew lived in the house for a short time after Cruz died in 1985, at the age of 103. It looks like the nephew just walked away one day.

As I examine the house, Pat catches me up on events in the neighborhood and the water association. Finally a new water system is in the works, something I tried to initiate for many years. That's good news for every homeowner in Chimayó. But Pat points out to me another kind of modernization that is not quite so welcome, at least among some people. Mounds of freshly dug earth and piles of dead tree trunks follow the low ridge marking the location of the Acequia de los Ranchos. Long stretches of fence line have been torn up, too. Pat explains that the ditch association decided to put the acequia in an underground pipe a few years back. They brought in heavy equipment last year to do the trenching and in the process tore up a lot of ground and destroyed fences and vegetation.

Pat says he can understand the desire to put the ditch in a pipe. It's getting ever more difficult to muster the labor to maintain the acequia. But he bemoans the destruction to the fences and laments that his cows can no longer meander over to the open ditch to get a drink. He has a harder time finding water for them.

Chris and Nancy have also expressed displeasure at the change in the ditch. They, too, resent the damage to their fences, and they also are very distressed to see the cottonwoods along the ditch slowly dying. The loss of the old trees is a consequence few foresaw, it seems.

A chill settles in as the sun goes down and Pat and I walk back across the fields toward his house. When we approach his cows grazing near the edge of a pasture, he cautions me to watch out for a young bull among them. I fancy myself experienced in dealing with feisty livestock, so I don't pay much heed, but then the bull lunges toward me. Pat shouts at him and waves his arms, but the animal circles and comes at me from behind. I didn't believe the bull would actually harm me, but now I'm not so sure. He ignores Pat and closes in on me. Pat hurriedly opens the strands of barbed wire to let me escape. The bull pulls up short as Pat curses at him in Spanish. "*¡Vete, cabrón!*"

Doorway on Patricio Cruz's house, 2010.

DICHOS ABOUT TRUTH

A cada capillita se le llega su funcioncita.
    Every little church has its little feast day. (Every dog has his day.)

El tiempo es buen amigo y sabe desengañar.
    Time is a good friend and knows how to reveal the truth. (The truth comes out in the end.)

La cárcel aunque sea de oro no deja de ser prisión.
    Even if the jail is made of gold, it's still a prison. (Freedom does not derive from wealth.)

La verdad es como el maíz—cuando uno menos piensa, sale.
    The truth is like a grain of corn—when you least expect it, it sprouts. (Truth is sometimes surprising.)

Lástima de tanto brinco estando al suelo tan parejo.
    Too bad there's so much hopping around when he's on a flat floor. (Said when someone is guilty of something and makes excuses before he has even been accused.)

Lo mismo está el cabo que la hacha.
    The handle is the same as the ax blade. (It makes no difference.)

Los locos y los chiquitos dicen la verdad.
    Crazy people and little children tell the truth. (Inhibitions can obscure the truth.)

No hay quien escupa a los cielos que a la cara no le caiga.
>No one spits to the heavens without it falling on his face. (If you curse God, there will be consequences.)

No le busques pies al gato porque le hallas cuatro.
>Don't go looking for the cat's feet, because you will find four. (Don't go looking for trouble, because you might find more than you bargained for.)

Nomás él que carga el costal sabe lo que trae adentro.
>Only the one who carries the sack knows what is inside. (Nobody knows your troubles except yourself.)

Nomás la lengua mata.
>Only the tongue kills. (Language can cause much evil.)

Ojos que no ven, corazón que no siente.
>The heart will not feel what the eyes do not see. (What you don't see won't hurt you.)

Vemos la paja en el ojo del vecino y no la viga en el nuestro.
>We see the straw in the neighbor's eye, but not the log in ours. (We notice even the smallest of other people's faults but seldom see our own, more significant ones.)

Narciso Trujillo, Los Ojuelos, 2010.

Narciso Trujillo in Los Pachecos

Hacen más unos callando que otros gritando.
There are those who accomplish more being quiet
than others who are shouting.

For years I've wanted to have a talk with Narciso Trujillo. I did speak briefly with him once, some years ago, when I lived near him. I watched him cross an empty field near my house each day, leading a swaybacked old horse on his way home in the evenings. After observing this daily trek for several months, I walked over to Narciso's house, an old adobe that intrigued me because of its antiquity and hand-built construction and because there was no road leading to it. Narciso had no need for a driveway, because he didn't have a car.

Back then, I found Narciso sitting in the sun by his gallinero (chicken coop). He spoke to me only in Spanish and obviously knew a lot about the old days. I intended to go back, but one day he stopped walking by our land, and I noticed a mound of freshly turned earth near his route. Later I learned Narciso's old horse had finally collapsed on the daily walk and was buried on the spot. Narciso moved from his house not long afterward.

Since then, I've moved away, too, and haven't seen Narciso, but I have heard his health is failing. In fact, someone told me he had lost his sight and was staying with his sister, where her children could watch after both siblings. They said he probably wouldn't be able to say much if I did talk to him. So when I began visiting Esequiel Trujillo, I asked how I might meet up with Narciso, who is his primo hermano (first cousin).

"*Ya no vive en su casa.*—He no longer lives in his house," Esequiel confirmed for me, along with the fact that Narciso was losing his sight. "*Vive con su hermana allá cerca del arroyo.*—He lives with his sister over there by the arroyo." When I asked for directions, he elaborated in Spanish on a number of turns down the road, across the Acequia de la Cañada Ancha and the arroyo, and finally, up a hill by a yellow house.

"*Es muy fácil.*—It's very easy," he assured me.

Now I'm trying to find Narciso's sister's house, and Esequiel can no longer advise me. He died last September, while I was away being a vagabundo again. I missed the *velorio* (rosary wake), the funeral Mass and burial, and the family gathering. It stings, especially when I remember the kindness and thoughtfulness of his last farewell to me, before I left on my trip.

I know this arroyo well but can't quite remember the directions Esequiel gave me. At the first trailer home where I see signs of life, I stop and tiptoe around a pit bull on a chain, who regards me suspiciously but makes not a sound—which I find more unnerving than a snarling dog. No one answers when I knock at the door, but just as I'm driving away, a man in a white T-shirt emerges and shuffles toward me. I stop and roll down the window.

"*Buenas tardes,*" I call out over the sound of the idling engine. He replies the same. Sticking with Spanish, I tell him I'm looking for Narciso and understand he's living with his sister somewhere nearby.

"*Mi tío Nars,*" the man says, smiling, and introduces himself as Juan Montoya. Squinting against the brilliant noonday sun, he explains to me how to navigate to Narciso's sister's house. "Go back to the pavement and follow the arroyo until you get to all those trailers, just before the school. Turn across the arroyo there, and go up a little bank and then up to the right. It's right there," he says.

The uneven bed of the arroyo jostles me along as I drive across it. This is the Arroyo de los Alamos. I once lived beside it, much higher up, where it enters Chimayó. I've seen torrents flood it during summer rains. It must be impossible for Narciso's people to get home during these times. Beside the arroyo here, there's a high mound of earth covered with branches intertwined with tires, and discarded objects of all sorts. I'm taken aback by the debris pile but then surmise it's been placed here as a barrier against high flood waters. Behind the haphazard levee stand a tight cluster of houses and trailers and, jammed among them, a small corral with two horses and a tiny wooden cage holding rabbits. This must be the place.

As I orient myself I realize I'm only a short distance from Juan's house, where I just got directions. He's just a stone's throw away up the arroyo, but the difficulty of getting down the eroded bed forces vehicles to take the circuitous route I just followed.

In front of two houses that form the nucleus of the compound, a bright green fifties-era Chevy gleams in the sun beside a defunct Grand Prix. An old man stands outside, ax in hand, in front of an enormous pile of split firewood. He wipes his brow and regards me placidly. I recognize Narciso. He hasn't changed much in fifteen years, and I guess he's not blind or bedridden, as I'd been warned.

Narciso wears a plaid shirt, heavy flannel jacket, overalls, a tall, broad-brimmed hat, high boots, and jeans held up in part by suspenders and in part by a belt cinched up tight. This seems to be much like the outfit he wore when I spoke with him years ago. His face bristles with a gray stubble of a beard. Leaning on a cane, he grins at me with a welcoming but bemused expression and holds out his hand, chuckling.

Narciso doesn't recall our conversation at his gallinero. I'm not surprised. But when I tell him where I lived (next door to his niece), he does remember my place and seeing me there.

"*Esequiel me dio direcciones para llegar aquí.*—Esequiel gave me directions for getting here," I tell him.

"*O, sí,*" he replies.

"*Me dijeron algunos que usted había perdido la vista.*—People told me you had lost your sight," I say.

"*O, sí,*" he says, smiling more broadly still.

I point to the pile of wood and ask if he split it himself.

"*Sí, poco a poco.*—Yes, little by little," he says, proudly.

He seems to need his cane while standing, but moves easily when he walks. To get out of the glare of the sun, Narciso ambles to the portal of a house near the woodpile. He stands, one hand on his cane and one on a battered enameled kitchen woodstove. After a few minutes, he sits down on a kitchen chair whose rotted seat has been replaced with a couple of pieces of weathered plywood.

In a while the November air begins to chill us both, so he goes over to a ragged old armchair facing into the morning sun and sits down. I remember noticing by the gallinero at his own house several easy chairs placed strategically in sunny and shady spots of his property. He's done the same here. I imagine him moving from chair to chair throughout the day, depending on the temperature, thermoregulating. Beside the chair he's chosen now, a used tire leans against an adobe wall plastered with concrete but never finished with a color coat. He's the picture of relaxation as he lists to starboard, still regarding me with an expression of amusement.

We begin with the family names. With a series of nods and *O, sí*'s, he confirms he's a cousin to Esequiel and brother to Magdalena, Grandma's former student and our dear friend, who died just last spring. Another sibling, Abel—whom Magdalena raised—passed on not long before.

Narciso slouches comfortably in the sun as I tell him of my close connection to Magdalena and my acquaintance with Abel. Narciso nods and says, "*O, sí.*"

Narciso is a man of few words. But, I remind myself, "*Hacen más unos callando que otros gritando.*—There are those who accomplish more by being quiet than others who are shouting." And, on the other hand, I can think of many people, unlike Narciso, who fit the dicho "*Es más lo que habla que lo que dice.*—He talks more than he says."

Narciso shakes his head and looks down when I mention Esequiel, who has been dead only a couple of months. Esequiel and I had talked about visiting Narciso. I wanted to put them together and let the old stories flow, but it never happened.

Narciso bears scant resemblance to Esequiel in appearance or manner, although they were primos hermanos. Narciso is quiet, inscrutable even. Bright, watchful eyes and an ever-handy laugh belie his age, which I guess is about the same as Esequiel would have been—mideighties. When I ask him how old he is, though, Narciso just laughs and says, "*No me acuerdo.*—I don't remember." He has the same reply, in words and chuckle, when I ask who his and Esequiel's grandfather was.

"*¿No se acuerda?*—You don't remember?" I ask, to be sure. But he doesn't recall his grandfather's name. I should know it, because Esequiel told me; he and Narciso descend from the same Trujillo from Rincón, whose brother married my great-great-aunt. This makes Narciso and me distantly related, too, at least through marriage. When I tell him this, he lets out another little laugh.

We're between Esequiel's neighborhood, called Los Ojuelos, and closer to a neighborhood sometimes called Los Pachecos. I've seen the name on a map, and it's mentioned in our papers, wherein José Ramón Ortega y Vigil (my great-great-grandfather, who was justice of the peace) registers a complaint from "*la placita de los Pachecos.*" (In this case, typical of the many José Ramón heard, José Lázaro accused a certain Ramona Salinas of infuriating him with *palabras groseras*—crude language—to such a degree that "*era una sin vergüenza y ladrona*—she was shameless and a thief." Lázaro asked José Ramón to restrain Ramona from making these verbal attacks.)

When I ask Narciso if he's heard of the plaza called Los Pachecos, he shrugs and says no. Plazas bearing surnames usually are named after the predominant family in the area, but I know of few people with the family name Pacheco living in the vicinity now. This place-name seems to be on the verge of disappearing, joining the ranks of countless Santa Cruz Valley names that few people, if any, recognize anymore. The old papers mention many of these, such as La Milpa del Llano, El Serrito de la Cruz, Barrancos Negros, Los Llanitos, Bosque de Ciruela, La Lagunita, El Charco, and many others.

A "Hello!" comes from down the driveway, called out by a man who emerges out of the collection of buildings and trailers surrounding us. He sounds suspicious and is clearly being protective of Narciso, but he's friendly and open when he reaches us and shakes my hand. He asks who I am and introduces himself as Telesfor, Narciso's nephew.

"You taking pictures of my Tío Nars?" he asks. I affirm that I am, explaining I've been making photographs, especially of older people, all over Chimayó. I open up a box of photos in the car to show him.

"Wow, these are beautiful. *¡Mira, mi prima Magdalena!*—Look! It's my cousin Magdalena!" he says, seizing upon a picture of Magdalena. "*¡Y primo Esequiel!* Can I have these?" he asks, and I assure him he can.

A woman with blond hair and blue eyes emerges from the house behind Narciso. She shakes my hand shyly and tells me her name, Betty. She's Telesfor's sister, Narciso's niece. I've heard of her; Esequiel told me she was taking care of Narciso and his sister—although the idea that Narciso needs care seems farfetched at this point. But Narciso never had children, and he is getting on in years. The rationale for having him move in with his sister María was that it would be better for him to have family around than for him to stay alone in his aging adobe. And since Betty was taking care of her mom already, having her tío in the house would be little extra bother.

Betty turns to studiously looking at the photographs Telesfor is pawing over. Then Israel, another family member, appears. He's young, slender, and bespectacled, a nephew to Telesfor and Betty. They call him Junior, since his father is named Israel, too. He cordially shakes my hand and then plants himself in another of Narciso's easy chairs, this one in the shade of a battered old apricot tree. He watches me closely, sucking thoughtfully on a Tootsie Pop.

A small voice drifts up the driveway, along with a whinny from Telesfor's horse in the corrals. A young girl comes running, bouncing a basketball.

"*Esta es my nieta, Alissa.*—This is my granddaughter, Alissa," Telesfor says, beaming like only a grandparent can. "*Mira, 'jita.* This man is taking pictures of Nars."

Alissa reaches out her hand, then gives Nars a little hug and sits on the ground against the wall, sunning herself. Narciso regards her with the same curious gaze he gave me when I arrived. Alissa announces she wants to be a famous singer and commences to sing for me, a pop song I've heard on the radio.

"Hey, I want to show these pictures to Mom," Telesfor says. "Come on in and meet her."

Narciso leads the way under a small portal and through a well-worn screen door into the house where María, Narciso's sister, lives. Faux wood panels line a dark interior, lit by a single bulb and by the glare from a television on which an old western movie is playing. There's an easy chair in one corner and a couch draped with a bright blanket. A simple print of the Last Supper hangs on one wall. Swaddled in blankets, María reclines in a La-Z-Boy. She stirs when we come in.

Smiling broadly and saying, "*Mira, mamá*—Look, Mom," Telesfor hands María the photographs. She makes a small sound of approval. He introduces me as "Don Usner, from the Ortegas of the plaza," and she nods that she remembers la Benigna and the others. She doesn't talk, but forces smile-like expressions as she takes my hand and grips it lightly. Her slight frame disappears in the folds of the blankets. Remarkably, she has few wrinkles and no gray hair. Telesfor tells me she is older than Narciso, but it can't be by much.

Telesfor explains to me that María, a Trujillo by birth, married his father, Manuel Montoya, forging a link between the two large families. Manuel died in April of last year. Tele asks me to take some pictures of his mom and his Tío Nars, and he coaxes the two of them mug for me, María lifting her head from the recliner, Narciso leaning over and smiling, with his hat still on. With some effort, María manages a bright smile, too. Then Narciso moves to the couch, where he's joined by his Chihuahua, Brownie, who's been growling at me suspiciously the whole time.

DICHOS ABOUT LOOKS AND APPEARANCE

Afeita un sapo, parecerá mancebo.
> Shave a toad, and he will look like a handsome youth. (Appearances can be deceiving.)

Caballo chiquito, siempre potrillito.
> Small horse, always a colt. (A petite person always looks younger than a large person.)

La cana engaña y la arruga desengaña.
> Gray hair deceives but wrinkles tell the truth. (You might get gray hair prematurely, but wrinkles will always reveal your age.)

Si no hubiera malos gustos, pobrecitas de las feas.
> If there were not bad taste, pity for the homely. (Homely people are fortunate that there are those who appreciate them despite their looks.)

Vale más fea y con gracia que linda y sin ella.
> Better to be homely and charming than beautiful and without charm. (Beauty is skin-deep.)

Ya está viejo Pedro para cabrero.
> Pedro is too old to be a goatherder. (Said of older people who are too ambitious.)

Ya no se compone ni con jabón de La Puebla.
> That can't be fixed even with soap from La Puebla. (Said of something that is so dirty or illegal, it can't be made clean.)

Ya no se le compone el ojo a la tuerta.
> It's too late for the one-eyed lady's eye to be fixed. (Said of someone who tries hard to be attractive, to no avail.)

Interior, Capilla de Santa Rita, Chimayó Abajo, 2010.

The Capilla de Santa Rita in Chimayó Abajo

A cada capillita se le llega su funcioncita.
Every little church has its little feast day.

For years I've admired a small chapel in lower Chimayó, a lovely white building atop a solitary hill near "the last arroyo," the one that roughly defines the western edge of Chimayó proper. Beyond the arroyo the highway passes through pastures that many years ago belonged to El Güero Mestas, my great-great-great-grandfather (a blond-haired, blue-eyed Irishman who was adopted into a Santa Cruz family in the nineteenth century), and then enters the realm of the next small community in the valley, La Puebla. The capilla is something of a landmark at the margin of Chimayó.

The chapel stands out prominently, despite its small size, and something about its location—so near to the settled valley yet removed, on the hill—gives it an air of particular grace. Like the San Antonio chapel in Potrero, it occupies an ideal spot, with a heavenly view. It's a place reserved for things of the spirit, humbly claimed by a shrine to a holy figure, in this case Santa Rita.

I remember noticing the capilla when I was a young boy passing by on our drives to Chimayó and wanting to climb up to it. Later, when I first rode my bicycle to Chimayó from Los Alamos, I watched for it to let me know I was nearing the end of the long journey. I've never known who owns the capilla, though, or how to get to it. It's on the periphery of my familiar world in Chimayó, deep in the lowlands among the *abajeños*, the lowlanders, as Grandma called everyone from lower Chimayó. Today, determined to find a way to reach it, I'm venturing down the valley in the late afternoon, hoping to catch a view of the capilla in the rich sunset light of this winter day.

I drive down Highway 76 past all the parts of Chimayó familiar to me, watching for public roads leading toward the chapel hilltop. Only one points in that direction, and I take it, dipping off the highway into an arroyo. Most roads in Chimayó started out as arroyos, which were the easiest way to traverse the terrain. This is no exception. The dirt track begins in the sandy bed and then climbs out, leading northward. Driveways branch off left and right, ending at trailer homes. I turn up the one closest to the hilltop and knock on the trailer door.

A thirtyish woman cracks open the door. I introduce myself and quickly explain I'm trying to get access to the capilla on the hill. She glances at me and says she's not sure who owns the chapel, but she invites me inside, smiling and saying, "I'll call someone to find out." She offers me a can of Coke and a seat on the couch next to a child who is watching cartoons on TV. A plastic Christmas tree in the corner shimmers with blinking lights. I sit next to the girl, who eyes me with wonder. The woman dials a number and asks a neighbor about the capilla, but gets no information. So she calls her brother.

"Hi sweetheart," she says with a touching warmth and affection; she's obviously very close with her sibling, who lives just down the road. But he's not sure who owns the chapel, either. This surprises me. It's right there, in their backyard, and it seems like everyone would know. I hear the brother's voice say, "*Pueda que el Dan sepa.*—Maybe Dan knows."

The woman directs me to Dan's house. Dan used to own a liquor store at "the last arroyo," so everyone knows him. More significantly for me, he also owned Bernardo Abeyta's house in Potrero. I've watched Bernardo's house decay slowly over the years, wishing I could intervene to restore it. Bernardo was, after all, the founder of the santuario and my great-great-great-great-grandfather, too, and his house stands on a hill overlooking the church. But Dan didn't have the resources to repair it and eventually sold the house to the Catholic Church, which has let it slip ever closer to ruin.

I pull up at Dan's brick house on the highway. Smoke trails from the chimney, and there's a car parked nearby, but no one answers when I knock. After several minutes, another knock, and a toot of the horn on my truck, I give up. But just behind his house I notice a driveway leading toward the chapel hill. I take it and steer to a house with a car in its carport. It's a sixties-era house, probably of adobe but modern in its lines, with a pitched roof and a statue of the Virgin in front.

I knock on the door, and immediately a voice calls out from inside, "Come in!" I'm surprised the occupant of the house wouldn't even ask who I am or have a look at me. Thinking she must assume I'm someone else whom she's been expecting, I call back, "But you don't even know who I am."

"¿Qué importa?—So what?" comes the reply. "Come on in."

I push open the glass outer door and then the interior door to the kitchen. Two elderly women are seated at the kitchen table, a box of KFC and some giant soft drink cups in front of them. They seem delighted to see me and remain seated, completely relaxed, as if I were a son home from college. I introduce myself, and they tell me their names, Nolia and Elena.

Nolia and Elena are sisters, from out near Tucumcari. Nolia married Leopoldo Martínez from Chimayó, now deceased. This is her house. Before marrying, she and Elena shared the family name Chávez, and the fact that I have Chávez blood arouses considerable curiosity and leads to the foregone conclusion: we're primos, however distant.

Eventually we get around to the purpose of my visit, although it now seems secondary to just getting to know these warm and friendly women. I ask about the Capilla de Santa Rita, and Nolia says, "Oh, just take that road there, go right up. My niece lives there. She takes care of the chapel."

"Are you sure it's all right?" I ask.

"Sure, she won't mind," Nolia assures me. So, leaving my truck alongside her car in the carport, I grab my backpack and tripod and head into the fields toward the road leading up the hill. When I'm halfway across the field, a pack of dogs charges out from a neighboring yard by a double-wide trailer. They put on quite a show of ferocity, and, feeling defenseless in the open, I hurry toward a fallen cottonwood, thinking to jump up on the trunk and brandish my tripod to ward the beasts off. But they pull up short, stopped by the deep acequia, now dry, that parallels the fence line in front of me. A few shouts from me, and they run back to their turf beside the double-wide.

The cottonwood log makes a convenient bridge across the ditch, and as I cross, it occurs to me I don't even know the names of the acequias down here. I'm feeling out of my element. In much of the rest of the valley, I at least know something about who lives where and how the water flows, but here I know not a soul. I'm also still not so sure Nolia has the authority to send me trespassing on the neighbor's land. So it startles me when I see a young man walking down the road toward me. I prepare to explain myself, but he just walks past me with barely a nod. Flummoxed by his nonchalance, I call after him, "Do you live here?" He stops, turns around, and says yes, he does, offering no further information. So I press him: "I'm trying to get to that chapel on the hill. Nolia said I could come this way. Is it OK?"

He stops and turns to me again, saying, "Sure. You can go either way around this hill and then up."

"But that way, I'll run right into a house. I don't want to bother anyone," I say, noting that one route leads smack into a house and corrals at the base of the chapel hill. He just shrugs and continues on his way.

Unsure of which way to go, I resolve to split the difference and climb directly up the hill in front of me. This will bring me to a hilltop across from the capilla, an ideal vantage for photographing it in the evening light. Abandoning the roadway, I climb up the steep spine of the hill, scrambling for footing in the sandy soil studded with round river cobbles. It's my intention to be discrete, to avoid drawing attention, but my efforts are in vain. Stones tumble down from my footsteps, and a blue heeler leaps to attention beside the house and corrals, now directly beneath me. His yapping carries far and wide, and he won't stop, even when I veer out of his view.

After several minutes of incessant barking, the heeler quiets at the command of a woman emerging from the house. She hollers up to me, "What are you doing up there?"

"I want to take pictures of the chapel. The neighbor over there told me it was OK."

"Who told you? That's my place."

"Nolia did."

"Well, who are you and what are the pictures for?" she yells, but politely. I explain myself, tell her my name, and mention I used to live by the old plaza. She pauses, then says, "Well, OK. I just like to know who's on my property. And my name is Alex."

"I'll come see you on the way down," I offer.

"It's OK," she says. "Just be careful up there."

"For sure," I reply. "But I am going to stop by. I want to meet you."

I continue to the crest of the hill, hurrying now to catch the golden light flooding the valley. It won't last long, since the sun is about to drop into a thick

Capilla de Santa Rita, Chimayó Abajo, 2010.

bank of clouds hanging over the Jémez Mountains to the west. The view from the top of the hill is everything I imagined: the Santa Rita chapel gleams like a beacon atop the small hill in front of me, behind it the entire valley—barrancas and farm fields and cottonwood bosques—leading up to the deep blue folds of the mountains.

It's preternaturally warm for a November evening, and I'm sweating from the climb. Managing a few photos before the sun sinks behind the clouds, I linger for a while, turning to the west to notice a crude gash of a road leading up the hilltop behind me. On top, a clutter of wrecked cars and discarded machinery accompanies a beat-up trailer home silhouetted against the sky—another blight that contradicts my theory about hilltops being reserved for places of worship.

I'd much rather not see the mess on the hill to the west, so I turn back to gaze to the east, where the chapel stands. The clouds quickly swallow the sun, and the golden light is gone, so I decide to walk over and ascend to the capilla itself, to have a look at it close up. Packing up my gear, I climb down the slope, heading for a low point to the east. Halfway down I notice, well hidden in the valley between the two hills, a cruciform building with a tall white cross in front. It's obviously a morada, a meeting place for Los Hermanos.

Descending the final slope of the hill, I circle the morada, staying at a distance out of respect. The front door of the morada is leaning open, and beside it a bit of graffiti stands out on the gray plaster. Instead of profanity, the spray-painted lettering reads: Love Christ.

I'm drawn to a small grave at the foot of the cross in front of the building. The largest marker bears the name Pedro Fresquis. A light bulb goes on in my mind. Grandma spoke often of "mi Fresquis," referring to her mother's stepfather. She never mentioned his first name; it was always just "mi Fresquis," but Grandma recalled that Pedro Fresquis was a brother to "mi Fresquis" and that Pedro used to provide her grandmother with firewood. Later, a Pedro Fresquis's daughter, Bernardita, married my grandmother's cousin, José Ramón Ortega, better known as Joe. My mom was at the wedding at Don Pedro's house when she was nine years old, in 1931. I've even seen a photo of some of the wedding party at the house, and now I realize that the photo was taken just a short distance from here.

Also, the Fresquis family name crops up several times in our documents. Apparently, the family used to own land in the Plaza del Cerro area. One records a land sale in 1838 from María Antonia Fresquis ("a resident of Chimalló") to Luis Ortega for fourteen *pesos de la tierra*. An 1855 document certifying the public right of way around the plaza also names a Fresquis.

A sloping trail leads to the top of the sandy hill. Just as I reach the capilla, the sun bursts out below the cloud bank, and the yellow light of evening floods the valley. The capilla's white walls glow warmly. The tiny building faces west, into the setting winter sun. Two whitewashed posts hold up a small portal and frame a dark wooden door. The bell of the capilla hangs in an enclosed, plastered belfry. A wooden six-pointed star, marked with Christmas lights, leans against one post; a power cord runs down the hill several hundred feet to the nearest house and electric outlet.

The chapel is a compact, tidy structure, humble but elegant. Inside, an

Morada, Chimayó Abajo, 2009.

altar-like cabinet, flanked by two archangel figures, holds up rows of statues. Images of the Virgin predominate, presided over by Santa Rita on a central dais, with stems of bright red plastic roses on either side of her. I find few male figures and only one large image of Jesus, a bas-relief of his face hanging on the wall above the santos. A similar bas-relief of the Virgin hangs on the opposite side of the altar. A wood structure for kneeling stands in front of the cabinet, on top of it a notebook where visitors can sign in and record their thoughts and prayers.

I thumb through the pages of the book to find a blank page. The most recent entry, written in large letters with a blue pen, reads simply, "Help Us!!!"

A broad swath of brilliant light pours through the doorway to fall just below a statue of a reclining baby Jesus. As the sun sinks still lower, it shines more directly on this figure, and I wonder if this is by design. Christmas is just weeks away, and it seems the doorway alignment is perfect for directing the sunset light onto the Christ Child and Santa Rita.

Santa Rita is the patron saint of impossible causes, of damaged wives and children, especially those abused by men in authority. I have no idea why the builder of this capilla (probably Pedro Fresquis) dedicated it to Santa Rita. I'm musing over these thoughts when the sun sets and the light quickly fades. I fold up my tripod and walk down the hill toward Alex's house, where I can see her in the yard with other people, gathering up goats and shooing them into the corrals for the night. Long before I reach the house, the blue heeler, barking fiercely, darts out to intercept me. I ignore him, which has the desired effect of disarming him.

Alex is visiting with her cousin Andy Apel and his children, who have the responsibility of corralling the chickens and goats for the night. They're having a tough time with a recalcitrant billy but finally coax him in, with the help of the dog, Azul. The cautious introductions Alex and I started as shouts continue amicably amid the bleating of goats. In no time, it's clear we are indeed connected in some way through the Fresquis line. I'll come back with my mother in tow, I tell her, to sort out the tangles in this connection.

CONSEJOS (COUNSEL OR ADVICE)

A la mala costumbre, quiébrale la pierna.
    Break the leg of a bad custom. (No mercy for bad customs.)

A la mala maña, se le corta un brazo.
    Cut the arm off a bad habit. (No mercy for bad habits.)

A la tierra que fueres, haz lo que vieres.
    When in another country, do what you see. (When in Rome, do as the Romans do.)

A quien te da el capón, dale la pierna y el alón.
    To one who gives you a capon, give her the leg and a wing. (Share your gift with the donor.)

A tu tierra, grulla, que esta no es tuya.
    Go back to your home, crane, for this land isn't yours. (You are far out of place.)

Al que madruga, Dios le ayuda.
    God helps him who gets up early.

Cada loco con su tema y yo con mi terquedad.
    Each nut with his argument and me with my stubbornness. (Said when an argument seems to have no end.)

Carne que crece no puede estar, si no mece.
> He can't be a person who grows if he doesn't swing. (He can't be a successful person if he doesn't take time to have fun.)

Cobra buena fama y échate a dormir.
> Earn a good reputation and go to sleep. (No need to praise yourself if you are praiseworthy.)

Con buenas palabras no hay mal entendedor.
> With good words, there is no one who misunderstands. (Speak well and you will be understood.)

Con paciencia, se gana el cielo.
> With patience, heaven is gained. (Patience is golden.)

Cosa platicada mal echa y desbaratada.
> A thing talked about is badly done and wasted. (Talking about what you are planning to do will ruin your plans.)

Cuando estés en la abundancia, acuérdate de la calamidad.
> When you are living in plenty, remember about calamity. (Never take abundance for granted.)

Cuidados ajenos matan al burro.
> Someone else's business kills the donkey. (Minding someone else's business will come to no good.)

De noche todos los gatos son pardos.
> At night all cats look gray at night. (Some people dress fancily, others plainly, but they are equal in status.)

Del cielo a la tierra no hay nada oculto.
> From heaven to earth, there is nothing hidden. (There are no secrets under heaven.)

Del dicho al hecho hay gran trecho.
>There's a long distance between saying and doing. (Easier said than done.)

Después de conejo huido, piedras al sabinito.
>After the rabbit flees, rocks hit the juniper tree. (It's too late to do anything after you've let opportunity pass.)

Después de cuernos, palos.
>After horns, sticks. (After deception comes the punishment.)

Después del burro muerto, maíz para el burro, ¿para qué sirve?
>After the donkey is dead, what good will feeding him corn do? (It's too late to fix the damage done.)

Dónde hay letras, callan barbas.
>Where there is knowledge, old men hush. (A learned person makes old men fall silent.)

Él que adelante no mira, atrás se queda.
>One who doesn't look ahead is left behind. (Keep your eyes on the road.)

Él que da pan al perro ajeno pierde el pan y pierde el perro.
>One who gives bread to someone else's dog loses the bread and loses the dog. (Don't waste your time or energy giving help to strangers.)

Él que en el alba se levanta pierde lo mejor del sueño y con su sombra se espanta.
>One who gets up at dawn loses the best of sleep and is frightened by his own shadow.)

Él que le duele la muela, que se la saque.
>If your tooth hurts, pull it out. (Get rid of what is bothering you.)

Él que sale a bailar pierde su lugar.
>One who gets up to dance loses his place. (If you don't attend to your business, someone else will take it.)

Él que tiene tienda, que la atienda, y si no, que la venda.
One who has a store should either manage it or sell it. (Take care of your own business or give it up.)

El tiempo perdido no se recobra.
Time wasted is never recovered. (Time's a-wastin'.)

En agua revuelta, ganancia del pescador.
Muddy water is to the fisherman's advantage. (Take advantage of unfavorable circumstances.)

En boca cerrada no entra mosca.
A fly cannot enter a closed mouth. (You'll stay out of trouble if you keep quiet.)

En la conformidad está la felicidad.
Agreement brings happiness. (Conformity takes away stress.)

En la ciudad de los ciegos el tuerto es rey.
In the city of the blind, the one-eyed man is king. (A person with even a little knowledge rules among the ignorant.)

Hay moros en la costa.
There are Moors on the coast. (Trouble is on the way.)

Hombre prevenido vale por dos.
One man prepared is worth two.

Hombre prevenido, nunca vencido.
A prepared man is never defeated.

Más vale ser cabeza de ratón que una cola de león.
It's better to be the head of a mouse than the tail of a lion. (You're better off as the brightest person among those of your class than as the lowliest among people who outclass you.)

No puede atender a la palma y al guaje.
> You cannot attend to the palm and the gourd at the same time.
> (You lack the skill to do two things at the same time. A reference to Matachines dancers, who use a palm and gourd in some of their dances.)

No se puede repicar la campana y andar en la procesión.
> You can't be tolling the bell and be in the procession. (You can't be two places at one time.)

No te fijes en culecas, fíjate en las que están poniendo.
> Don't concentrate on the brooding hens; pay attention to those that are laying eggs. (Pick the single girls, not the married ones.)

Un bien con un mal se paga.
> A good deed is paid with a bad one. (No good deed goes unpunished.)

Vale más llegar a horas que ser convidado.
> Better to come in time than be invited. (Better to show up at mealtime than wait to be invited.)

Vale más mal vendido que mal perdido.
> Better to sell it cheap than not to sell it at all.

Vale más tarde que nunca.
> Better late than never.

Vale más un pájaro en la mano que cien volando.
> A bird in the hand is worth a hundred flying. (A bird in the hand is worth two in the bush.)

Ya más claro no canta el gallo.
> The rooster can't crow any more clearly. (The message can't be any clearer.)

Tom Montoya, Los Ojuelos, 2010.

Tom Montoya and the Maytag Roller

Él que al pobre cierra la puerta, la del cielo no halla abierta.
One who closes the door on the poor will not find
the gates of heaven open.

It's a warm January day. I slip into the driveway at María and Narciso's place and encounter a man I haven't met before, standing on the sunny side of the building (*la resolana*) where I so often find Narciso warming himself. He introduces himself as Tom Montoya, Narciso's nephew. He holds back a minute, until he notices the camera around my neck, at which point he says, "Oh, you must be the guy who took the pictures of my mom and tío!" He extends his hand, and I join him in the resolana, taking in the sun. Tattoos decorate his exposed forearms, and he wears a silver cross around his neck; it gleams brightly against his black sweater. A black headband holds back a shock of silvered hair that tapers to a ponytail, matching the color of his wispy beard. Tom's bright blue eyes regard me warmly.

"We really like those pictures, man," he says, leaning back against the wall. I ask him about himself. He grew up right here, he tells me, went to high school in Española, then was off to Vietnam, where he served as a medic.

"It was heavy, let me tell you," Tom says. "I saw all these guys who were really messed up. Had to try and patch them together. I'm still dealing with it."

Tom is one of five children of María. Their father died just two years ago. María is not doing so well. But the family is rallying around her, with three taking the lead in caring for her. Tom is one of those three and proud of it.

He asks about my family and stops me when I tell him my grandmother's name.

"You're Benigna Chávez's grandson? That was your grandma?" he asks and then says, "Eee, I know her! From up there at the plaza, no? I bought her washing machine!"

"No," I say. "You're kidding. You're the one who got her old machine?"

"Yes, in 1980. I heard she was selling it and went over and picked it up for a hundred bucks. I figured it was a good price, you know."

"That old machine with the rollers, the Maytag?" I ask.

"Yes, that's the one."

"I used to do laundry on it when I was little," I tell him.

"I still use it, in the summer," Tom says.

"Where is it?" I ask, and Tom leads me behind his house, just down the driveway. He pulls off a couple of old handmade rag rugs, and there it is, the old Maytag with the rollers, looking just like it did when Grandma had it inside her screened porch. There's no rust on it, and Tom says it still works fine.

One of my chores at Grandma's was to feed clothes into the wringer—a task that always frightened me because I was sure the rollers would suck my fingers in and mash them flat, like the towels, socks, and other items that passed through. After wringing the clothes, I'd help hang them on the rickety clothesline in the patio. And then came my favorite task: dumping the leftover water from the machine onto the red-ant hills that continually cropped up in the driveway. I would hook a garden hose to the machine and direct the flow onto the mounds, sending the ants into a feverish rage. Each time I was sure I had eliminated them for good, but the next morning they would be back, as if nothing had happened.

I remember when Grandma sold the machine. She regretted it for years. Afterward, she had to rely on others to take her laundry to town to wash it for her.

We return to the resolana. Betty, Tom's sister, comes out of María's house to see what's happening, and then Telesfor walks up from his place. They line up for photos against the wall, three of the five in the family. Next, Lawrence, Betty's partner, appears. I've met him here before.

All of us chat about family names and ancestry, searching for family relations that the Montoyas and my family hold in common, but we come up empty-handed. Although I can't find records of Montoyas living around the

Plaza del Cerro in our documents, the Montoya family name shows up in an 1809 land sale of eighty-two *varas castellanas* from José Franciso Montoya to Juan Bautista Vegil, for the price of *"una mula de camino y dos bacas paridas y dos pesos en rreales y dose pesos de la tierra.*—one walking mule, two cows lately delivered, two pesos in coin, and twelve 'pesos de la tierra,'" a quasi-monetary unit indicating an exchange of agricultural products in lieu of currency. Additionally, several Montoyas were signatories to an 1825 land sale (one of them, Severiano, as alcalde of Santa Cruz de la Cañada).

Tom asks if I know how to copy photographs. He has a picture of his parents he'd like to duplicate for his siblings. Lawrence enters the house he and Betty share and comes out with the picture, a photocopy of Manuel and María's wedding photo, framed in coarse pinewood with the bark still on it. Smoke has stained the photo, but the youthfulness and joy of the young newlyweds shines through. Tom and Lawrence hold it up for me to photograph, and I promise to make some copy prints for them.

Lawrence is a Medina from Potrero, where my mom's grandfather was from. Lawrence knows many of my distant cousins in the Chávez family there, but what's most remarkable for him is the realization it was my uncle, Bobby Chávez, who saved Lawrence's brother from drowning in Santa Cruz Lake, sometime during World War II.

"Bobby was your uncle? Really? He was there that day, one of the kids in the boat, and the only one who could swim. He managed to pull out my brother Frankie, but he couldn't save Rafelito. But Bobby—he was a hero, man! I heard he died a few years back."

I remember the story well. As Bobby told it, he tried to rescue Elías's son Rafelito too, but he couldn't. Poor Rafelito was all tangled up in branches or rope or something. But the good karma from Bobby's deed still resonates. Any friend or relative of Bobby Chávez is a friend to the Medinas and to many others in Potrero, even though the incident happened decades ago and Bobby is long gone.

Tom Montoya and the Maytag Roller

DICHOS ABOUT WORK AND MONEY

Buscando trabajo y rogando a Dios no hallar.
    Looking for work and begging God not to find any.

¿Dónde va a ir el buey que no are?
    Where can an ox go that he does not have to plow? (A laborer will always be stuck in menial jobs.)

El dinero del mezquino anda dos veces el camino.
    The miser makes his money travel the road twice.

El trabajo es virtud.
    Work is a virtue.

Él que ha de ser real sencillo aunque ande entre los doblones.
    Small change will remain small change even if it is mixed with big money. (A poor person will always be poor, even if she associates with the rich.)

Él que no trabaja, no avanza.
    One who doesn't work doesn't get ahead.

La pereza es llave de la pobreza.
    Laziness is the key to poverty.

Lo barato cuesta caro.
    Cheap things end up costing plenty.

Lo que puedas hacer hoy, no lo dejes para mañana.
    Don't leave until tomorrow what you can do today.

Más da el duro que el desnudo.
    The stingy person gives more than the penniless.

No es oro todo lo que relumbra.
    All that glitters is not gold.

No hay atajo sin trabajo.
    There's no shortcut without work.

No hay bolsa más quieta que una bolsa sin dinero.
    There is no purse more still than a purse without money.

Nomás las orillas y el medio me faltan.
    Just the ends and the middle are left to do. (Said when you haven't even started what you are supposed to do.)

Unos son los de la fama y otros son los que cardan la lana.
    Some have the fame and others card the wool. (Some get the credit while others do the work.)

Vale más una gotera seguida que una chorrera de repente.
    A steady drip is better than a sudden gush.

Tom Montoya in his Matachín traje as the Monarca, 2010.

Wolfie and Another Corona

La esperanza no engorda, pero mantiene.
Hope doesn't fatten you, but it maintains you.

It's a bleak, cool spring day, and it hasn't snowed in a long time. The bare trees are already desperate for water, and the long, dry months of May and June lie ahead for the battered and gray land. The light is washed out, and the wind has been blowing incessantly for weeks. Smoke puffs from the stovepipes of all the houses. Spring is a season of little promise here; the greening won't come until the rains arrive in July.

I'm taking my daughter, Jennifer, with me today to visit Narciso and María. I have pictures to drop off for them, and Jennifer has to complete an assignment in her photography class. As we arrive, Betty comes out of her house to greet us, and then Tom emerges from María's house, followed by another sister, Cruzita, whom I have not met before. They all greet us with smiles, and Cruzita steps up and gives Jennifer a huge hug. I can tell Jennifer feels at home already. The three siblings gather around the photos of Narciso and María I've brought, then Betty steps aside and leans against an abandoned washing machine, grinning at a small puppy wagging down the dirt driveway toward her. The dog is irresistible as only puppies can be, with fluffed-out fur and a tiny black nose. Everyone in the family is taken with the new pet, but none so much as Betty. She beams from ear to ear. The puppy makes the rounds, dashing from one adoring fan to the next. Jennifer has found the subject for her photos—and for all of her attention.

As I'm chatting with Tom, I learn he used to dance with the Matachines under Esequiel's direction. In fact, he and the group danced in the Plaza del Cerro once. Tom kneels in the dirt to draw a map of where they danced.

"Yeah, we danced there in the plaza in . . . I think it was '98, and we even brought Tía Grabielita. We went for her in Ranchitos."

"Wait," I butt in, "Grabielita is your tía?"

"Yes, through my wife. My wife is a Vigil from Cundiyó."

"You mean she's related to all those Vigils up there, like Esquipulas, Noberto—all those?"

"Of course, those are her primos. Her name is Valeria."

"*¡No me digas!*—Don't tell me!" I say. "They're parientes of mine, too."

"Yes, and I have a cabin there, right by the river, you know by the bridge? That's ours. Oh, I love it up there in Cundiyó."

The puppy runs over to Jennifer, and she bends to pet him.

"That's Wolfie," Tom says. "The mother is supposed to be a wolf. From the mountains. He's part wolf and part husky."

Getting back to the Matachines, I ask Tom if they are dancing in Chimayó anymore.

"No, not here," he says. "We don't have any more dancers in the group. Some became druggies—and it's too bad, because the whole reason to do the dances was to keep people away from drugs. We even had a speaker come to the group to talk about drugs.

"But before, when we were together, Esequiel was the leader, and he was a good dancer. Oh, he would jump!" he continues. "And I mean . . . at his age? To jump like that? He was about seventy-five then, maybe older, and he would jump about five feet in the air! And he would go like this, 'Ooo, ooo!' at the Abuelos." Tom crouches down, then leaps up, waving his arms in imitation of Esequiel. "He would make us all laugh. Oh, he was a character!

"And I knew Esequiel's father, Don Benigno. He was my uncle, my grandpa's brother. He was a chiropractor, but he told me never to be a chiropractor because it was too hard of a life."

Telesfor approaches me and hands me a can of Coke.

"When people would go to Don Benigno's house, he would not charge them," Tom continues. "He would tell them, 'Just throw whatever you want in the cup.' And that's how he would make his living."

I tell the joke about Benigno reaching high up on the old ladies' knees, and Tom convulses with laughter, saying, "That would be my Tío Benigno!

"But who is your father?" Tom asks me.

"My father was a gabacho," I tell him, using the New Mexican Spanish word for a person of foreign origin—basically a kinder, gentler synonym for *gringo*. "His name was Arthur Usner."

"Well, how did you come to . . . what is your last name?"

"Usner, but my mom is Chávez."

"Are you related to . . . he's gone now, Tony Chávez? Or Nestor Chávez?"

"Yes, Nestor was a cousin to my grandma."

"OK, and what about Leví?"

"*También*. All those Chávezes from Potrero are cousins."

"Then who is your uncle from Potrero?" Tom presses me.

"Well . . . my grandma's name was Ortega, but she married a Chávez, Abedón, and he was an only child of—"

Lawrence Medina walks up and Tom points to him and says, "His father and mother were from Potrero, like the Chávezes. He's a Medina. But what I want to know is how the Abeytas came to build the santuario in Potrero." I start to tell Tom what I know about the santuario, but Lawrence turns the conversation to the photos of Narciso and María I brought, telling me he likes them in color much better than the black-and-white versions I gave him earlier this spring.

Tom jumps back in to talk about the Matachines dances, telling me the history of the dances and the symbolism of the various accoutrements of the dance.

"The *guaje* or gourd rattle symbolizes peace, and the palma trident means trade between the Spanish and the Indians—things like corn. They say they had the corn first, but we brought the corn, we brought the gold, we brought the silver. There was none of that here. They had the turquoise, yes. And so we became friends through trade, and then our dance, we passed it on to them. We gave them our dance, the Matachines."

"And what's the story in the dance?" I ask.

"It's about good versus evil," he explains. "Like, in the dance I'm trying to protect the Malinche, which is the Virgin Mary. And my warriors, they're going to help me, because evil is going to come, the Beast, which we call the Torito. And the Torito is at the hand of the Beast, the Torito. Until we—"

Lawrence walks up and puts his arm around Tom, saying, "This here is my *cuñado* [brother-in-law]—or will be some day, when Betty and I get married. But we're not going to make no wedding party."

"So, the Abuelo kills the Beast," Tom continues, "the little Beast that's after the Virgin Mary. And the warriors all jump to finish killing the—"

Lawrence walks over again, holding up a picture of María I gave to Tom. Tom struggles to continue.

"See, the Monarca, he's the captain of the whole dance. He's like Cortés. That was Esequiel, when he was still dancing."

"And who's Malinche?" I ask.

"The Malinche, she was Betty when she was small," he responds. "She represents the little Virgin Mary. Like *mi Señora de Guadalupe*, that's what we use the capes for."

Lawrence holds up another of the prints I made, of Betty, Cruzita, and Tom with María on her bed, and he says something about how much he likes it. Tom keeps talking.

"And the Monarca, he directs the warriors to show them how they're going to fight. In one hand he holds the palma, the three-pointed thing, to ward off the evil, and in the other hand he holds the guaje, which means peace. That thing is so old—it was passed on to me by the Romeros from La Cuchilla. Let me go bring it so you can see."

Tom walks off to fetch the guaje and the palma.

"Lawrence, did you ever dance with the Matachines?" I inquire.

"No, I wouldn't know how," he says, farcically imitating a dancer. "But maybe Tele knows," he adds, pointing to Telesfor.

"No, I never danced with the Matachines, but Betty knows how."

Betty, sitting on an old washing machine behind me, brightens into a bashful grin.

"Did you dance with the Matachines?" I ask her.

She nods, blushing, and Telesfor calls out, "Show us a few steps."

"I know how, but I don't want to," she demurs.

Narciso emerges from the house, smiling at me.

"*¿Cómo está su hermana?*—How is your sister?" I ask.

"*Está bien.*—She's fine," he says, nodding.

"*¿Y ya se bañó usted?*—And you just took a bath?" I ask him, noticing his hair is still damp. He laughs heartily.

"*Ya.*"

Narciso wears his usual plaid shirt, suspenders, and beat-up cowboy hat, but today he's also sporting what appears to be a necklace of round wooden beads.

"*Oiga, yo quería saber quiénes eran sus papás.*—By the way, I wanted to know who your parents were," I say, wanting to fill in a blank in my knowledge of the family genealogy.

"*O, Pulita se llamaba, y Valentín.*—Oh, my mother was Pulita and my father was Valentín."

"*¿Y de dónde vino la Pulita?*—And where did Pulita come from?" I ask.

"*Yo no sé dónde sería.*—I don't know where that would be."

"*Y el apellido de ella?*—And her maiden name?"

"Vigil."

"*De Cundiyó?*—From Cundiyó?" I ask, knowing Cundiyó is the source of many Vigils in Chimayó.

"*No. De aquí, de Chimayó.*—No. From here, from Chimayó."

"*Y su papá era hermano a don Benigno, ¿qué no?*—And your father was brother to Don Benigno, right?"

"*Sí. Hermano a Benigno y Calletano.*—Yes, brother to Benigno and Calletano."

"*¿Y por qué trae usted un collar hoy?*—And how come you're wearing a necklace today?"

Betty, Telesfor, and Tom break out in raucous laughter.

"That's his rosary, man!" Tom says. "We just started Lent yesterday, Ash Wednesday, and he always wears it this time of year. He was a Penitente, you know."

At this juncture, I return to genealogy and inform Narciso that I found out his grandfather's name by calling my friend Aaron, who has tracked the genealogy of many families in Chimayó, and by reviewing my notes from a conversation with Esequiel. Narciso seems pleased to recall the name, Guadalupe Trujillo.

Betty calls me over to a table out beside the apricot tree, where she's placed a small black-and-white photo of three people standing in front of an old Chevy truck.

"This is the picture I want you to copy."

"Oh, who is it?" I query.

"*Mi padrino.*—My godfather," she answers, pointing to a figure on the left. "Lupe Trujillo. And my brother, Rudy."

"And who's that?" I ask, half-jokingly because obviously it's Betty when she was younger.

"That's me."

"With glasses? I've never seen you with glasses."

Betty lays out another photo, much older. In this picture, two children pose in front of a black backdrop, the smaller child seated in a wooden chair and the taller standing alongside.

"That's my mom," Betty says, pointing to the smaller child, now the woman grown old and lying in bed in the house beside us.

Tom returns, holding up the palma, and says, "Look—just imagine how old this is." He also holds out a gourd rattle (the guaje) and a colorful corona, similar to the one Esequiel showed me. Tom's is decorated with a row of bangles that, when I look closely, I realize are made of pop tops from beer cans.

"I have another one, too," Tom says. "And my daughters have the other ones at home. And I have the story of the Matachines right here."

Tom opens a spiral notebook and begins to read from several pages of cursive writing describing the Matachines dance and its history. He used these notes, he explains, to introduce the dance when he performed in it.

"The Matachines dance, considered a sacred dance offering praise, honor, homage to our creator . . . this dance is known to originate from Spain, on or before 1598," he reads while Lawrence, Betty, Narciso, and Telesfor listen attentively. "The dance became multicultural when Cortés married a Mayan Indian . . ."

I contemplate correcting Tom by pointing out that La Malinche was actually Nahua, and not Mayan, but I want to hear the story as he understands it.

Tom puts down the notebook and dons the corona, announcing, "I'm going to show you a little bit of the dance. *Quita el perro.*—Move the dog away," he says to Betty, who scoops up the puppy to get him off the patio. He begins to shake the rattle and dance in the driveway, explaining his movements as he goes.

"You step, step, cross the palma and the guaje like this, then turn . . ." He demonstrates the choreography, dancing and twirling past Narciso's easy chair, the washing machine, the emerald-green Chevy. Jennifer, wide-eyed, watches with the others while a couple of dogs snooze, unimpressed, and Wolfie yaps incessantly from the cage where they've placed him.

"And that's the way it goes. It's a beautiful dance. I wish I had the music, to really show you."

Breathing hard from the exertion of dancing, Tom talks about how the dance group fell apart. A major blow to the group was the death of one of the main dancers, who died of a heroin overdose.

"Esequiel wasn't happy about that," he remarks. "But we kept on dancing, for Tío Esequiel. And then, now just before he died, he wanted one dance, one more dance, but his wishes weren't granted."

"Well, I was talking to Esequiel," I related to him, "and he said he wanted his niece to organize the dance and make it happen last Christmas before he died, when she came to visit. But for some reason it never happened."

"Well, maybe you could talk to Esequiel's daughter and find out when the niece is coming next, and we could dance. I don't know where, maybe even here," Tom says, gesturing to the driveway where he just demonstrated for me. "You talk to her."

Tom changes the topic abruptly to Los Hermanos. Pointing to Narciso, who is leaning against the washing machine, Tom says, "*Este hombre y mi daddy eran Penitentes. ¿Era hermano, no?*—This guy and my daddy were Penitentes. You were a brother, weren't you?"

Narciso nods.

"*Usted es Penitente. ¿Hermano de la morada?*—You're a Penitente? A brother in the morada?" I repeat.

Narciso nods again.

"*¿De cuál morada?*—From which morada?" I inquire.

"*De aquel abajo.*—From that one, below," he answers, pointing northwest.

"*¿De la morada de Pedro Fresquis?*—You mean Pedro Fresquis's morada?"

"*No, no, no. Aquí. De aquí del Llano.*—No, here, here in El Llano."

"It's all graffitied already," Tom adds. Then he asks Narciso, "*¿Hay tres Penitentes allí 'hora, no?*—There are three Penitentes there now, right?"

"*No, dos no más. Remigio y Mañuel.*—No, only two, Remigio and Manuel," Narciso responds.

"*O, sí, ya murió el Deagüero, y el Jerry también.*—Oh, that's right. That Deagüero died, and Jerry, too," Tom remembers. "*¿Pero con usted son tres, ¿no?*—But with you, there's three, right?"

"They seal themselves in the morada, and they don't come out during Holy Week," Tom says to me, "except they're allowed maybe five hours to come visit the family. And they eat only bread and fish during that whole time."

"*¿Entonces usan la morada esa todavía?*—So they're still using that morada?" I ask Narciso.

"*Sí, todavía.*—Yes, still," he replies.

"*¿Y mañana van ir a rezar, cantar, y todo?*—And tomorrow they'll go in to pray and sing and all that?" I ask.

"*Sí, mañana,*" Narciso answers.

"It's very sacred," Tom adds. "They won't even let me in there."

"*Yo quisiera tomar fotos de los Penitentes, pero no me dejan.*—I'd love to take pictures of the Penitentes, but they won't let me," I say jokingly, for I know full well that Los Hermanos are very protective of their privacy, so much so that some call them a secret brotherhood.

"*¡No, no le dejan!*—No, they won't let you," Narciso says, bursting into laughter.

"*¿Y cómo es ser Penitente?*—And what's it like to be a Penitente?" I ask. "*¿Es muy duro?*—Is it pretty tough?"

"*O, sí,*" Narciso replies.

"You have to learn all the alabados," Tom interjects, referring to the hymns of praise practiced by Los Hermanos, especially during Easter.

"*¿Y conoce usted a los alabados?*—And you know the alabados?" I ask of Narciso.

"*Sí.*"

"*Pues, cánteme uno.*—Well, sing me one," I suggest.

Narciso looks at Tom and back at me and laughs energetically at the suggestion.

"*Cántele ese de las horas de la noche.*—Sing him the one about the hours of the night," Lawrence says, joining the conversation.

"*Tío. Dile el Padre Nuestro.*—Uncle, say the Our Father for him," Betty says.

"*Cántele un alabado.*—Sing him an alabado," Tom insists.

"*O, échale un tequila por cantarla.*—Oh, give him a shot of tequila to sing it," Lawrence chimes in.

"*Haga un rezo no más.*—Just say a prayer," Tom says. By this point I regret suggesting he say anything at all about Los Hermanos, and I certainly hope a bottle of tequila doesn't emerge. Nars seems confused and unsure of what to do. But at the same time, he's tickled to have the limelight. Tom tries to jump-start him by beginning to intone the Our Father in a droning voice. Narciso laughs nervously and then begins to recite the prayer himself. As he finishes and launches into a Hail Mary, Tom interjects, "*Ándale, pues.*—

Go for it," and he continues to insert short comments into Narciso's recitation of the prayer, like rap fans encouraging a rapper's spontaneous lyric.

When he's done, Tom says, "I was in the Penitentes for three years, but I was a punk. Three years." Then turning to Narciso, he continues, *"De veras, ¿no? Yo, David, Rudy y Tony, nomás tres años juntamos, ¿te acuerdas?*—It's true, isn't it? Me, David, Rudy, and Tony, we just met for three years, remember?"

"*Sí.*"

"It was something you had to be there for, but we were party guys. So we couldn't last. We were young. Eleventh, twelfth graders. We wanted what was out there in the streets: party. We weren't faithful to the morada. You have to be very faithful."

"*¿Ya no hay jóvenes en la morada?*—There are no young men in the morada now?" I ask Narciso.

"*No, no hay. Puros viejitos.*—No, none. Just old men."

"*Quizás es la única morada que queda en Chimayó, ¿no? Porque la de abajo, del Pedro Fresquis, ya no se usa.*—I guess that's the only morada left in Chimayó, because the one down there, Pedro Fresquis's morada, is no longer in use," I comment.

"*Ya no.*—No longer," Narciso affirms.

"Since Vicente died—he was the president," Tom adds, "and Leroy, he lives right over here, he was the vice president, but he goes to the morada in Los Ranchos now; and then Román, well, he died, too. So then they closed it, and now they graffitied it."

"*Lástima.*—Too bad," I say, and Narciso nods his head in affirmation: "Lástima."

DICHOS ABOUT LOVE AND FAMILY

Donde no hay amor no hay fuerza.
   Where there is no love there is no will. (Love motivates everything.)

El amor se va a donde quiere, no donde su amo lo envía.
   Love goes where it wants to, not where its master sends it. (Love has its own will.)

Él que quiere al col quiere las hojas de alrededor.
   One who likes the cabbage likes the leaves around it. (Once married, you must love not only your spouse, but also your spouse's family.)

Duele más dedo que uña.
   A finger hurts more than a fingernail. (Said when someone takes the side of an immediate family member in a fight among relatives.)

La primera es escoba y la segunda, señora.
   The first woman is a broom and the second, a lady. (The first wife is treated like a servant and the second, as royalty.)

La sangre sin fuego hierve.
   Blood boils without fire. (Blood is thicker than water.)

No hay cuña más mala como la del propio palo.
   There is no wedge worse than that which comes from your own tree. (Said of one who makes trouble within the family.)

Si la vaca es ligera, la ternera va adelante.
> If the cow is fast, the heifer is faster. (If the mother sets a bad example, the daughter is even worse.)

Vale más un yerno del infierno que una nuera de la gloria.
> It's better to have a son-in-law from hell than a daughter-in-law from heaven.

Ya es harina de otro costal.
> She's now flour from another sack. (Said when a young woman gets married and leaves home.)

Vale más viejo conocido que muchacho por conocer.
> Better an older man you already know than a young man you have yet to meet.

Angel statue, road to Chimayó, 2012.

Grabielita on La Pascua

No hay mejor experiencia como la que el tiempo da.
There is no better experience than that which time gives you.

It's Easter Sunday, *la Pascua*. Gone are the throngs of pilgrims who made their way to the santuario two days ago, on Good Friday—a day when we generally avoid visiting Chimayó. The carnival atmosphere of the pilgrimage contrasts dramatically with the way it used to be, the way we liked it. The sheer volume of traffic, on foot and in cars, along with the noise and clamor, makes it nearly impossible to get through Chimayó, much less sink into feelings of reverence and introspection. So Mom and I waited until today to come visit.

Not that the Good Friday experience at the santuario doesn't offer some sustenance. In fact, I "made the walk" this year, or almost made it. My sister Janice and I set out from Cundiyó, where she lives, intending to make the pilgrimage cross-country, completely away from the roads and crowds. I wanted to take her up over the summit of Tsi Mayoh, the hill whose Tewa-language name was the origin of the Hispanicized word *Chimayó*. We also planned to stop at the Cueva del Chivato, a small cave on the hill's flank that Tewa cosmology describes as a place of contact with subterranean spiritual energies. Janice had not been to either place.

We started walking at the bridge in Cundiyó at 7 a.m. on Good Friday, and we were immediately enthralled by the morning light on the hills above us as we worked our way downstream. The rushing Santa Cruz River, as high as it would get this year from snowmelt, roared in the rocky gorge. Eventually the footpath ran out, and we were blocked by cliffs and the still water of Santa Cruz Lake, created by the dam of the same name. We scrambled up steep, rocky hillsides for an hour or more, stopping now and then to admire the dramatic views of the foothills, the snowy peaks, and the deep, green Santa Cruz Valley. In the end we were thwarted by the sheer scale of the landscape and turned back toward Cundiyó, but we made a vow to blaze the cross-country route next year.

On our way back to Janice's home, we walked through Cundiyó, which clings to a hillside sloping down to the Río Frijoles. The fields below us, along the Río Frijoles, had greened fully and shone like emeralds in the narrow valley. We paused at the tiny Santo Domingo chapel to visit the gravestones of our ancestors in the courtyard: Longino Vigil, Gelacia Chávez Vigil, and Libradita Ortega Chávez. (Libradita's name is misspelled on the gravestone as "Libodita.") Libradita was great-grandpa Reyes's sister; Gelacia was her daughter, and Longino, her son-in-law. They link us to kin in Cundiyó.

But that was Friday, and now it's a much quieter Easter Sunday in Chimayó. The trash from the pilgrimage has been cleaned up and packed in tall plastic bags by prisoners on work release. As we pass the santuario, Mom describes the somber Easters of her childhood, when fully veiled women in black and men in black suits walked silently in procession, heads bowed, along the dirt road to the santuario. Then, there were only a few rough benches and a couple of chairs on the dirt floor of the church; most people carried small *pisos*, homemade rag rugs they knelt upon during the Easter Mass.

As we approach the turnoff to the santuario, Mom says, "Did I tell you about how Father Roca insulted Jamie the other day? He and Ruth went to talk to him, and Jamie said, 'Father Roca, ¿cómo está? ¿Qué no me conoce?—Father Roca, how are you? Don't you know me?' And Father Roca jokingly replied, 'O, sí, te conozco, ¡pero ya estás grande—y muy viejo y muy feo!—Oh, sure, I remember you, but now you're grown up—and really old and ugly!' Another time Father Roca said to Liliana, '¡Eee, cómo estás vieja!—Oh my, how you've aged!' He's really *travieso* [mischevious], Father Roca!"

It dawns on me we haven't discussed what we'll do in Chimayó today, so I ask Mom, "Where are we going, anyway?"

"I don't know," she says. "You were so anxious to come to Chimayó! There's too many cars coming to the santuario. I was thinking of stopping to see Father Roca, but I'm afraid to stop now. Father Roca might insult me, too!"

After some discussion, we decide to bypass the crowded santuario and instead call on Grabielita, whom I haven't seen for a couple of months and

Mom hasn't seen since last year. Last time I knocked at her door, she answered in her night clothes, nursing a terrible cold. Today there is a car in her driveway, so we assume she's up and around and visiting with relatives. But my knock on the door goes unanswered, as does the ring of the doorbell. I try a few times, giving Grabielita a chance to make her way to the door, but to no avail. Just as we're backing out of the driveway, though, the screen door opens and Grabielita's granddaughter, Peggy Sue, beckons us in, explaining she and Grabielita were taking a nap together. I apologize for disturbing them and say we'll come back, but she insists we come inside.

Peggy Sue leads us to the bedroom, where Grabielita is seated on a couch. She's happy to see us and takes my mother's face in her hands, while uttering her most common expression, a term she can inflect with many meanings: "*¡Linda!*" She says it with the e's drawn out—"Leeeenda"—and an intonation conveying much *cariño* (affection or tenderness). She takes my hand and repeats the word, in the masculine: "*¡Lindo!*"

Peggy Sue scrambles to get a brush and starts combing Grabielita's hair, all the while explaining why they were napping in the middle of the day. They had risen early to get ready for Mass and grew tired by midafternoon. Grabielita apologizes for her appearance.

"*O, todavía estás muy pretty pretty, Grandma.*—Oh, you're still very pretty pretty, Grandma," Peggy Sue says.

"*¿¡Qué pretty ni pretty?!*—What's this 'pretty pretty'?!" Grabielita responds.

"*Ésta es una nieta fina. Es puro oro.*—This is a really fine granddaughter. She's pure gold," Grabielita says of Peggy Sue, who fusses over her.

"*¡Ella es el oro!*—She's the gold!" Peggy insists, pointing to Grabielita.

"*¿Pues, del oro sale el oro, no?*—Well, gold comes from gold, right?" I add, and Grabielita agrees—"*¡Sí!*"—and lets out a cackling giggle.

Then Grabielita turns to my mother, continuing the conversation in Spanish.

"*¿Cuántos años tienes?*—How old are you?"

"*Ochenta y ocho.*—Eighty-eight," Mom replies.

"*¡Parece mucho a mi prima Benigna! Linda, linda . . . bien, bien parecida . . . el mismo retrato de tu mamá.*—You look so much like my cousin Benigna! Pretty, pretty, you look so much like her. You're the picture of your mother," Grabielita comments, smiling wistfully at Mom.

"*O, y el primo Abedón y mi viejo se querían como hermanitos. Esos sí se querían bien.*—Oh, and cousin Abedón and my husband loved each other like brothers. They sure cared for each other," Grabielita continues, referring to my grandfather. Then she asks, as she did on our last visit, how many grandchildren Mom has, and they go over the list of names.

"*¡O, sí, soy tatara-tatarabuela!*—Yes, I'm a great-great-grandmother!" Grabielita reminds us, laughing enthusiastically. "*¡Ayy! Esta mujer sí está vieja, linda.*—Ahh! That woman is old, my darling," she says, speaking of herself and making a mock grimace. "*Y mis nietos, ya grandotes viejos.*—And my grandchildren, they're good and old," she adds, giggling some more.

"*Ayy, linda. Pero no me duele nada, más de la vista 'hora. Esta semana pasada fui al doctor y me operaron. Y quedó bien, mira.*—Oh, but nothing hurts me, except for my vision now. Just this week I went to the doctor, and they operated on me. And everything came out fine, look," she says, gesturing to her left eye and removing her glasses.

"*Pero me dolió, linda.*—But it really hurt me, darling," she continues, modulating her voice up high and then down, expressively. "*De esto he pasado mal. 'Hora está bien, ¡pero muy reaguado!*—From this eye I've suffered a lot. It's OK now, but very watery!"

Then Grabielita turns to me and again says of my mom, "*¡O, mi prima Benigna! Eso le digo porque parece mucha la Estela a ella.*—Oh, my cousin Benigna! I tell this you because Stella looks so much like her."

Mom and I remind Grabielita that she's fortunate to be able to see, and she nods, but then makes a grieving sound and says, "*La única cosa es que leía tanto. Me gustaba mucho. Y 'hora no. Nomás que las letras grandes puedo ver. Ya no, lindo. Y era mi consuelo. Mis rezos y todo. Y 'hora . . . ¡Todo se acaba!*—It's just that I used to read so much. I liked it a lot. And now I can't. I can read only big letters. No longer, darling. It was my consolation. My prayers and everything. But everything passes!" she says as she makes a sweeping motion with one hand against the other.

"*La vejez es muy trabajoso, ¿no? Es muy feo. Muy feo llegar al viejito. Pero yo doy gracias a Dios. ¡Pero cómo se pasan los años!*—Old age is really difficult, isn't it?" she continues. "It's really terrible to become an old person. But I give thanks to God! But how quickly the years pass!"

Changing the subject, I tell Grabielita about my walk from Cundiyó on Good Friday and about seeing the gravestones of my relatives at the Santo Domingo church.

"*O, sí, era mi tío Longino.*—Oh, sure, that was my Uncle Longino," she comments, nodding. "*Y mi tía Gelacia.*—And my Aunt Gelacia."

Peggy Sue interrupts us, offering me a cup of coffee, which I accept.

"I have to warn you, this is pretty potent coffee," she says, gesturing toward Grabielita. "Grandma drinks it like this every day."

I sip the brew, as thick as motor oil.

"*¡Trailes cookies!*—Bring them cookies!" Grabielita directs Peggy Sue. Then she turns to Mom and shakes here head, marveling again. "*¡Lindo! ¡Mira cómo se mira a mi prima Benigna . . . ¡Prima Benigna le digo yo! Mucho, mucho se parecen. ¡O, la misma cosa!*—My goodness! Look how you look like my cousin Benigna! Cousin Benigna, I tell you! You look so, so much like her. The same person!"

Peggy Sue brings the cookies and looks at my cup of black coffee. "You sure you don't want sugar? That's gonna kick you pretty strong and keep you awake tonight."

"*¿Entonces Longino era tío a usted?*—So Longino was your uncle?" I ask, getting back to the topic at hand.

"*Sí. Era hermanito a mi papá.*—Yes, he was my father's brother," Grabielita responds.

"*O, allí es de donde viene la parentela.*—Oh, that's how we're related," Mom adds.

Grabielita counts her uncle's siblings on her fingers: "*Mi tío Longino, y mi tío Luis, y papá, y luego tío Félix . . . eran seis hermanos por decirle. Y mi padrino Isidro de Córdova. Se llamaba eso porque se casó con una de Córdova y ella se lo llevó para Córdova.*—Uncle Longino, Uncle Luis, my father, Uncle Félix . . . there were six brothers, to name them. Another was my godfather, Isidro of Córdova. They called him that because he married a woman from Córdova and she took him there," she recalls, letting out another giggle. "*Leeenda . . . Y de mujeres quizás nomás una tuvieron. Estaba como yo. Seis hombres y mujeres no tuvo más que a la Grace.*—Oh, my. And girls, they only had one, just like me. Six boys and no girls—except for Grace."

"*Sí, y mi tía Gelacia tuvo mucha familia también.*—Yes, and my Aunt Gelacia had a big family, too," Mom offers.

"*Sí, mi tía Gelacia tenía muchos . . . eran mi primo Lorenzo, primo Noberto, primo Pulas, primo Manuel Vigil, primas Rosarito, Demesia y Trinidad.*—Yes, my aunt Gelacia had a lot of kids . . . cousin Lorenzo, cousin Noberto, cousin

Pulas, cousin Manuel Vigil, and female cousins Rosarito, Demesia, and Trinidad," Grabielita recites as she munches on a cookie.

"*¡Y ya no leo, y era tan leydora! ¡Y también huevona soy! ¡Huevona, huevona!*—And now I don't read, but I was such a reader! And I'm lazy, too! Lazy, lazy!" she exclaims, smiling at Peggy Sue.

"I got her up and dressed and she said, 'You know, I just feel tired. I don't want to go.' And I said, 'You're the boss, so you get to decide. And it's OK . . . *Está bien, Grandma. Hicimos mucho ayer. Es bueno que descansas hoy.*—It's OK, Grandma. We did a lot yesterday. It's good that you rest today."

"*¡Huevona, huevona!*" Grabielita interjects, repeating her self-castigation, only half in jest, as she munches down another cookie.

DICHOS ABOUT CHILDREN AND CHILD REARING

Cría uno cuervos pa' que le saquen los ojos.
>You raise crows so they can pluck out your eyes. (Said when one's children are ungrateful or disrespectful.)

Él que tenga hijos en la cuna que no hable de mujer ninguna.
>He who has children in the cradle shouldn't go around talking about any woman. (A new father shouldn't be thinking about other women.)

En casa de gaitero todos son danzantes.
>In the house of the piper all are dancers. (Children follow their parents' example.)

En casa de herrero, cuchillo de palo.
>In the home of the blacksmith, a wooden knife. (The blacksmith can't afford his own products.)

Hijos crecidos, penas dobladas.
>Grown children, double worries. (Parents never finish raising their children.)

No es madre la que pare, sino la que cría.
>A mother is she who rears a child, not the one who bears him. (Nurture is more important than nature.)

Salió con una pata más larga que la otra.
> She ended up with one foot longer than the other. (Usually said when a woman has a baby out of wedlock.)

Sean como fueren, los hijos de uno duelen.
> You hurt for your children no matter how they turn out. (Children bring heartache as well as joy.)

Juanita Mestas's grave at the old cemetery, Potrero, 2009.

At the Campo Santo on Memorial Day

De la suerte y de la muerte no hay quien se escape.
From fate and from death, no one can escape.

It's sunny and hot—and windy—as my daughter Jennifer and I find our way amid the gravestones in the campo santo in Potrero to locate the markers for our dearly departed. I'm teaching her how to locate even the oldest ones I know, repeating to her name after name, hoping she's a faster learner than I have been. We stop first at the mysterious *sepultura* of Juanita Mestas, who died at the age of eleven and to whom I believe we're distantly related, although I'm not sure how. The wooden railing along one side of her plot has finally collapsed. I've watched it lean slowly downward for years. Untangling the weathered railing from cholla stems and tumbleweeds, I prop it upright. No one else has touched this grave site in years.

We walk carefully around the cactus and barely recognizable remains of grave markers to the small iron fence and white headstone at the sepultura of my grandmother's mother, Genoveva Archuleta Ortega. She died in 1919 while giving birth to the first boy among the nine children she "gave light to," as they say in Spanish (*a quien le dio luz*). I cut at weeds with a shovel and rake them away. As I tell Jennifer the sad story of her great-great-grandmother's death, she points to the grave beside Genoveva's, a tiny plot surrounded by halved concrete blocks. She asks who is buried there, and I get down on my knees and sweep away grasses and dirt to look at letters impressed in the concrete slab: A. Ortega. With a start, I realize it's the grave of Antonio, the last baby Genoveva birthed, who lived for about eight months after she died. I never noticed the grave before.

We wander to the newer part of the cemetery to find Grandpa Abedón's last resting place. Surprisingly, the Siberian elm I dug out last year has not returned, and the grave site needs almost no maintenance. As we do at all the graves, we calculate from the dates on the marker the age of the deceased. For Genoveva it was a mere forty-one years; for Abedón, only forty-eight.

We wander just down the hill from Grandpa's grave to that of his eldest son, Leo Chávez. Another sadly low number comes up when we do the math: forty-two years. He was one of my mother's two younger brothers, and I remember well when he died, the same year Martin Luther King Junior and Bobby Kennedy were killed, the year of the My Lai massacre. It was a devastating year.

Uncle Leo was a wildly mischievous child, Mom has told me, and he carried his rambunctious sense of humor into adulthood. Like his grandfather, Juan Climaco Chávez, Leo finessed his way by wit and charm and grit to become a high-rolling businessman. He built his company in Los Angeles, and every time he returned home to Chimayó he was a celebrity—especially when he flew in his private plane, but also each time he showed up in a new Cadillac. Leo unabashedly bought my devotion; every time I saw him, he pulled out a roll of bills and peeled off a five-dollar note for me, handing it to me with a pat on the head. It worked. I worshiped Uncle Leo.

I'm telling Jennifer all this history as we linger at Leo's grave, waiting for Mom and my brother Arturo, who are overdue for their planned meeting with us at the campo santo. A voice from a group of three people at a nearby grave calls out to me, "Can we borrow your rake?" and an elderly gentleman approaches me to get the tool, introducing himself as Rubén Montoya.

"Are you related to the Montoyas down the valley, Narciso and them?" I inquire.

"No, I'm not from here, but my wife is," he says, gesturing toward the older of two women at the site he was working on. "That's Nora, Nora Martínez. She grew up right over there," he says, pointing with his chin, "and she knows everyone around here."

"My mom has lots of relatives in this neighborhood," I tell him as we head toward Nora, who with her daughter, Linda, is pulling up cheatgrass from around a well-kept plot ringed with a railed fence, marked with a handsome headstone. Nora smiles as she looks out at me from under a broad straw hat. The first order of business is kinship, of course, and she points to the name on the headstone beside her: Crisóstomo Martínez. "This is my dad," she says, as if introducing the real person.

"Wow, that's amazing," I say. "Crisóstomo was my mother's great-uncle. She called him Tío Choto. I never knew him, but Mom has spoken of him often, describing him as '*muy travieso*,' very mischievous. In fact, just a few days ago she pointed his house out to me and told stories about him and his wife, Pablita." Nora smilingly affirms yes, that was her dad. She is as delighted as I am to meet another cousin in Chimayó.

"Oh, sure, I know your mom," Nora says when I tell her my mother's name, "but I haven't seen her in . . . forever. We were at Menaul High School in Albuquerque at the same time. My older brother, Elizardo, was best friends with your mom's brother, Leo. They used to hang around and stir up trouble together. I remember one time when they said, 'We're not going to wash our socks anymore. We'll just buy new ones,' and they went to Española and did just that."

Just as Nora introduces me to her daughter Linda, Mom and Arturo pull up and begin making their way toward us. Mom stops at Leo's grave but doesn't want to go the extra distance up to Tío Choto's, so I lead Nora down to her.

The smiles sparked by my mom's reunion with Nora are as bright as the spring day. They chatter on and on about the schools they both attended— John Hyson Elementary, just down the road, and Alison James Boarding School in Santa Fe, in addition to Menaul—and all their mutual friends and relatives, most of them gone.

Meanwhile, Rubén and Arturo and I chat beside the graves of Choto and Pablita, making occasional efforts to clean up the weeds. Rubén is a World War II vet, very active in veterans' organizations. He worked at the lab in Los Alamos for many years. "I worked with uranium, milling it and handling it in all sorts of ways, and I got cancer. But I beat it, thank God," he tells us.

"There was a lot of discrimination up there at the lab," he continues, "and I was very involved with fighting it and helping people from the Valley to get a fair shake. It was bad, sometimes—and hey, are you going to pay me for all those pictures you're taking?" he jokes.

I learn Linda is a photographer in Mesilla, and she and her parents have my books about Chimayó. "We love those books," Rubén says enthusiastically. I could never receive any kind of accolade or endorsement more welcome.

Rubén goes over to find a seat to rest upon, on the railing of a nearby grave. Linda and I compare our experiences as summertime visitors to Chimayó in our youth, discovering that, for both of us, spending time with the old people—along with freedom to wander at our leisure throughout the valley—topped our list of favorite things about visiting Chimayó.

"I love to come here with my parents," Linda says, affirming with the tone of her voice that we share the same kind of attachment to this place. "I love the smell of the rain in the summer and coming to the campo santo and checking on Grandma's house."

We look at her parents and my mom, sitting on the railing of the grave and chatting animatedly, and we know we will be here without them some day, as they lie behind these very railings or ones like them. We dread the day but will welcome the visits here, to place plastic flowers again and touch the earth of Chimayó.

The conversation goes on for a half hour, then a woman at a nearby grave calls out to me, "Can we borrow your rake?" I walk over and hand the rake to one of two sisters, who have already worked up a sweat and have quite a pile of grass, weeds, and spent plastic flowers left over from last year. I ask whose grave they're cleaning. "Leo Chávez's," the older woman replies.

"But I'm cleaning Leo Chávez's grave, too!" I say.

Amazingly, there are two gravestones bearing the name Leo Chávez, only a dozen feet apart, but none of us has ever noticed. I present my credentials—I drop a few names of relatives, that is—and, of course, Rosalie and Marcella and I are related. They are Nestor Chávez's daughters. Nestor's father was Manuel Chávez, who was married to Victoria, my great-grandfather Juan Climaco Chávez's niece. (His brother, Miguel, was her father.) Discerning this crazy quilt pattern of relationship entertains us for some time, and resolving its intricacies requires that we pull in the big guns—Nora and my mom—to put it all together.

I mention to Rosalie and Marcella that Nora is Choto's daughter. The two sisters light up and shout over to Nora, "Oh, so *¿mi tío Choto era su papá?*—Oh, so my uncle Choto was your father?"

"*O, sí!*" Nora replies.

"*Y era tío a mi mamá también.*—And he was my mother's uncle, too," I chime in.

"*Sí, pero más antes*, everybody used to call everyone 'tío,'" Marcella says.

"But this really was her tío," I point out.

Nora looks at the sisters and muses, "*Me acuerdo mucho de la mamá de . . .*

—I remember a lot about the mother of . . . ," and she trails off, unable to recall the name. Suddenly more interested, everyone draws close to try to figure out whom she's thinking of.

"*Estaba . . . la tía . . . ¿cómo se llama? La que murió pronto.*—She was . . . the aunt . . . what was her name? The one who died young," Nora continues, building up the mystery.

"It was her mother," she goes on, pointing across the campo santo in the direction of a hundred graves.

"Whose mother—La Nita?" Rosalie suggests. Nora nods no.

"La Epifania, or la Epimenia," Mom throws in. Nora purses her lips, shakes her head, and says, "No, *no está viva ella.*—No, she's not alive. *Mi tío Juan era su . . .* —My uncle Juan was her . . ."

"Juan Sandoval?" Marcella asks. "*¿Él que vivía allá cerca del santuario?*—The one who lived there, close to the santuario?"

"No, no. *Mi tío Juan Chávez era el esposo de ella.*—No, my uncle Juan Chávez was her husband."

I'm suddenly elated, for I can actually come up with the name.

"Adelaida!" I say, and Nora brightens and repeats the name excitedly.

"*Adelaida era mi bisabuela.*—Adelaida was my great-grandmother," I say.

After we talk about Adelaida a bit (how she suffered so when Juan lost everything in the Depression and they had to come home to Chimayó like beggars), the conversation winds down as the heat grows a bit too much to stand. Marcella and Rosalie hand me the rake, and Rosalie says, "*Bueno, pues.*—All right, then. Nice to meet you. I hope we didn't break your camera."

"Maybe I'll see you here next year," I reply.

"If we're still here," Rosalie says, laughing brightly.

"But if we're not here," I say, pointing to all of us in succession, "we'll be here," gesturing to the campo santo. Rosalie laughs again and says, "No, if we're not here, we'll be up there, at the new cemetery. There's no room for us here!"

Mom and Arturo and I say our good-byes to the crowd of parientes at the campo santo in Potrero, ready to move on to the newer Catholic cemetery, just up the hill. There we park by the graves of Grandma, who died at 103; of my nephew Jeremy, who died at 21; and of my grandnieces, twins who died at one day old. All are equally remembered. Mom whispers a few words about her mother—"We love you, Mama!"—and tears well up. Arturo and I stare, still in disbelief, at Jeremy's grave, right next to Grandma's, dug the same year.

At the Campo Santo on Memorial Day 215

The wind blows fiercely through the plastic flowers that we anchor in place with mounds of stones, knowing full well that they'll be scattered in spite of our efforts.

It's time to make our final stop, at the Presbyterian cemetery across the valley, on the land that once belonged to my great-grandfather Reyes Ortega. On the way, though, Mom insists we stop at Leona's Restaurante for her favorite treat: a *chicharrón* burrito. This simple burrito should be the poster image for heart disease: a flour tortilla wrapped around nuggets of pig fat deep-fried in lard. Mom loves them, as Grandma did. Mom remains hale and hearty as she nears ninety, and Grandma lived with this kind of diet for over a century. (Seeing the dripping burrito reminds me of when I first moved in with my grandmother, after I returned as an adult from living in California. Determined to "clean up" her diet, I made her eggs in a Teflon pan, using no oil. She looked at them and then ordered me to melt a generous helping of lard on them.)

When we get to the Presbyterian cemetery, Mom, limping heavily because of an injured knee, just manages to climb up the hill to Grandpa Reyes's stone. Reyes still holds a very special place in our hearts, even my brother's and mine, though he and I never knew our great-grandfather. Beside him, his daughter Juanita's stone notes she died on her birthday at the age of seventy-six years; I helped dig her grave, when I was a teen just out of high school. It was one of the last ones dug by hand in the cemetery. Next door on the sandy hillside lies another of Reyes's daughters, Melita, whom we loved dearly, and beside her, her husband, Isaias. And then another daughter, Petrita, whose sorrowful and painful last years we remember with deep sadness.

As we mosey from grave to grave back down the hill, Mom tells stories about the deceased buried in each one. So many graves, so many stories. We pause to listen to every one.

DICHOS ABOUT FAITH

A los bobos se les aparece la madre de Dios.
    The mother of God appears to simpletons.

Dios dice,—Cuídate que yo te cuidaré.
    God says, "Watch over yourself that I may watch over you."

Dios no castiga con palo ni azote.
    God doesn't punish with a stick or a whip. (God has subtler ways to punish.)

Dios no cumple antojos ni endereza jorobados.
    God does not fulfill whims nor straighten hunchbacks. (God does not concern himself with petty or selfish requests.)

Dios resiste a los soberbios y da gracia a los humildes.
    God denies the wise and gives grace to the humble.

Dios tarda pero no olvida.
    God might take his time, but he doesn't forget.

El hombre propone y Dios dispone.
    Man proposes and God decides.

El pan partido, Dios lo aumenta.
    God multiplies bread that is shared.

Él que no habla, Dios no lo oye.
    He who doesn't speak, God doesn't hear.

Él que por otro reza, por si aboga.
    He who prays for another pleads for himself.

Él que sabe una oración, nomás se acuerda y la reza.
    One who knows only one prayer has only to think of it and he recites it. (One who has a bad habit keeps repeating it.)

Esperando el bien de Dios sin saber por dónde viene.
    Waiting for the grace of God, not knowing where it will come from.

La esperanza no engorda, pero mantiene.
    Hope doesn't fatten you, but it maintains you.

No se acuerdan de Santa Bárbara hasta que hacen los truenos.
    They don't think of Santa Bárbara until they hear the thunder. (Some people don't remember to pray to Santa Bárbara—the patron saint of thunder and lightning—until they find themselves in trouble.)

Para el santo que es la misa, con un repique sobra.
    You only need to ring the bell once for the saint the mass is being said for. (It is not important to dress up for a gathering that will be very casual.)

Si Dios no quiere, santos no pueden.
    If God does not will it, saints can't do it.

Ya aguantaron las velas, ¿cómo no aguantan los cabitos?
    The candles lasted this far—why shouldn't the stubs last? (If you have been able to bear your sufferings for a long period of time, you can bear them longer.)

Delfin Roybal, Plaza de los Dolores, 2012.

Tomasita's Green Chile

Él que hambre tiene, en comer piensa.
One who is hungry thinks only of food.

Tomasita's little dog runs out from under a pickup truck to yap at us, announcing that Mom and I have arrived. It's not the usual time of year for us to visit. Normally, we come in the fall for red chile, but we've had a hankering for some green this summer. In all the years we've been getting chile from Tomasita, we've not once tried her green chiles. We mentioned this to Tomasita a few weeks ago, and she invited us to come back when the chiles were ready. That time has come. Tomasita has picked a bushel for us from the first harvest.

Giant cumulonimbus clouds billow over the mountains and thunder rumbles softly in the distance as I get out of Mom's car and approach the dog. He growls as if guarding the bushel of chile in the bed of the truck, but he flees at my approach. The pods gleam, creating a halolike glow around the basket. I can smell them. Their fragrance, combined with the thunderstorm-charged atmosphere, evokes memories of roasting chiles on Grandma's woodstove. Green chiles and thunderstorms are the very essence of late summer in Chimayó.

I pick up a few chiles and bring them to Mom. She holds them, sniffs them, smiles. Tomasita emerges from her house and greets us graciously. It seems like just yesterday we were here getting red chile from her, but it's been almost a year. We ask about her health, her family; she asks about ours. And then we get to talking about chile.

"The thing about chile," Tomasita says, watching me as I snap a pod open and take a crisp bite, "is that once you start eating it, you can't stop. My kids are always coming over and I put out *cacerolas* of chile and they just devour it. And if I don't have any ready when they get here, they say, 'What happened to all the chile?' And I tell them, 'Well, the the other kids got here first and ate it all.'"

"Even my grandson, Delfín, he's crazy about chile, and he's only four. He takes a bite, and if it's too hot he blows in and out like this"—she puffs her cheeks out—"and then he takes a sip of water and then goes for another bite of chile."

We laugh about the chile addiction that grips so many here, including us.

"Oh, I grew up growing and eating chile," Tomasita relates. "*Pero ya casi no siembran.*—But now people hardly plant at all," she says. "They say, 'It's too hard. It's too much work. I don't have time. It's too much trouble.' But I notice it's never too much trouble to eat it!"

It's been a difficult water year, with water available to Tomasita from the Acequia del Distrito only every two weeks or so. She's managed by planting her chiles over near her son's house, where there is access to the Espinosa acequia, which comes directly from the Santa Cruz River in Los Ranchos. Between the two ditches, there's just enough water to keep her chiles going.

"The chiles love the hot weather we've been having, but they need water, too," she says. "This is the hottest, driest summer I've seen for years. It didn't used to be like this. You could count on the rains in the old days, and the ditches were usually running full. Not only was there more water; people took care of the water and land better in those days.

"Oh, how things have changed," Tomasita pines. "They've changed so much. It used to be so nice, with all the land around here planted and hoed and full of chile, corn, melons. Now it's just a pigpen. Nobody plants. They don't clear their land. Look over there. You can't even walk through, with all those thick trees. And your pants get full of stickers, if you manage get through. They don't even bother to take care of it anymore.

"And people don't take care of each other, either," she goes on. "My parents used to tell my sisters and brothers and me, 'Love each other.' And we learned that. If we'd get in an argument, we'd make up and say we're sorry and really mean it. I still talk to my brothers and sisters every day, on the phone. But nowadays, people around here don't even talk to their brothers and sisters! Not to mention their neighbors. Some people don't talk to anyone."

Tomasita looks over to my mother, sitting in the car, and says, "*Es que algunos, ¡ni solo se aguantan!*—Some people can't even stand themselves!" She and Mom laugh, and Tomasita goes on, "Jesus said we're all brothers and sisters, so we all need to love one another. But all people care about now is material things. People want more and more things, and then they die, and they have nothing at all.

"Nowadays people don't know how to eat, either. I remember when my father would buy a one-hundred-pound sack of flour, some coffee, potatoes, and that would last us for months, and we didn't have to go to the store. We had our own cows, pigs, chickens. We ate fresh eggs every day. We had tortillas made with whole wheat flour. And now if you give a kid a whole wheat tortilla, they don't like it. They say it has freckles!"

My mom nods in agreement and adds, "And then they talk about organic this and organic that, and they say lard is *so* bad for you. It used to all be organic, from right off the farm."

"Yes," Tomasita agrees. "I used to come home every day from school and my mother would make me a tortilla and spread it with a layer of fresh lard, from our own pigs, and it was good! And look at me! I'm still here and I'm still planting chiles, when all these young people say they're too tired to do it!"

Mom nods again. "And we never heard of diabetes, high blood pressure, heart attacks, strokes. And now they go to the doctors constantly, and they take pills all the time, and they die young—but they say we shouldn't eat lard or meat and all that. *¿Sabes qué? ¡Están locos!*—You know what? They're crazy!"

I'm still confused about how we're related to Tomasita, so I ask her and Mom to explain it to me again. This time the entire conversation takes place in Spanish, with occasional English phrases thrown in. I turn on a tape recorder and listen attentively, but I'm still lost. How many times will they have to go over this before I get it? I wonder. But at the same time I realize that Mom and Tomasita's dialogue is, in effect, a recital for them, so they won't forget.

My mom begins, "*Allí es donde viene la parentela, de Severo,* but *¿quién era el papá de Severo?*—That's where our kinship comes in, through Severo Martínez. But who was Severo's father?"

"*Epifanio era el papá de Severo.*—Epifanio was Severo's father," Tomasita explains.

"*¿Y luego cómo venía del lado tuyo?*—And then how did it come down to your side?"

"*Era del lado de mi mamá.*—On my mother's side."

"*Bueno, pues. ¿Tu mamá era qué de mi primo Severo?*—All right, then. Your mother was what to my cousin Severo?"

"*Severo era su tío de mi mamá, porque Severo y su mamá de mi mamá . . . eran hermanos.*—Severo was my mother's uncle, because Severo and the mother of my mother were brother and sister . . ."

And so it goes, with more lists of names and relations and memories of personalities. I've heard this before, but I haven't yet committed it to memory. Listening, I realize there is no end to this story of families and relations, and it's my task to keep telling it. I'm humbled by the realization.

The sun is sinking low when we get back into the car for the ride home, the green chiles filling the interior with their fresh scent, and lightning flashing from a black thunderhead on the western horizon. In my imagination I'm already tasting the green chile we'll make when we get home.

Thundercloud over the Jémez Mountains, ca. 1995.

DICHOS ABOUT FOOD

A faltas de pan, cemitas son buenas.
    When there is no bread, crackers are good. (When one is hungry, any food tastes good.)

A la mejor cocinera se le ahuma la olla.
    The best cook sometimes burns the pot.

Barriga de pobre, primero revienta que sobre.
    A poor man will rather split his belly than waste food.

Barriga llena, corazón contento.
    Full belly, happy heart.

Con hambre no hay mal pan.
    When one is hungry, there is no bad-tasting bread.

De lo que no cuesta se hace fiesta.
    From that which costs nothing, a feast is made. (Make the most of it when someone else is paying the bill.)

Donde no hay harina, todo es mohína.
    Where there is no flour, everything is sadness. (Without food, there is sadness.)

Él que hambre tiene, en comer piensa.
    One who is hungry thinks only of food.

Entre menos burros, más elotes.
>With fewer burros, more ears of corn. (There will be more to eat if fewer people are eating.)

Vale más que me haga mal que se pierda.
>Better it makes me sick than having it go to waste.

Barrancas, 2012.

Postscript

It's been six years since I started this journey of chasing dichos around Chimayó and decided to write a book about it. Of course, there's a dicho for that: "*Del dicho al hecho hay gran trecho.*—There's a long distance between saying and doing." In the case of this book, that is an understatement. There have been countless junctures when I've looked at this project and thought, "*Nomás las orillas y el medio me faltan.*—I'm just lacking the ends and the middle," a dicho that applies well to a seemingly endless task.

In those five years, much has changed. Besides Magdalena, Narciso's sister María, and Esequiel—all of whom died while I worked on this book—Grabielita has now passed on. I'm sure she is rocking Roger in her arms in *el cielo*. Nolia, Alex's tía who lived down by the Santa Rita chapel, is gone now also, and I regret that I didn't get a chance to spend time with her.

Lorenzo from the Plaza del Cerro was nearly killed when the senior citizen's van he was riding in collided head on with another car. (Lorenzo recovered and used his insurance money to buy a new Jaguar and a new Buick; the sight of them parked in front of his house on the old plaza was indeed odd.) When she heard that Lorenzo had survived the accident, Mom commented, "*¡Escapó la gallina más que sea sin pluma!*—The chicken escaped, even though it lost its feathers!"

The twins' father, Nick Trujillo, passed away suddenly, and his absence resonates in the plaza along with the hollow emptiness of abandoned buildings. As my mother remarked upon his passing, "*Que Dios lo tenga de una oreja.*—May God have him by one ear."

I was right about the beaver who had invaded the plaza. He turned up dead with a bullet wound in an abandoned cesspool tank a few months after I saw his handiwork there.

Tom Montoya, Narciso's nephew, has fallen gravely ill with conditions that he believes started with exposure to toxins in jet fuel in Vietnam—or perhaps to chemicals when he worked in Los Alamos—but he hangs on, carefully guarding his precious Matachín *traje*. He finally received the Purple Heart—a bit of reparation he has awaited for nearly forty-four years. (He also received monetary compensation, which he used to purchase a 2007 GT Mustang.) Tom's brother Rudy died at sixty-six after a long battle with leukemia; I remember last seeing him leaning uncertainly on his cane and surveying the great pile of firewood his eighty-year-old uncle had split. (Rudy danced as the abuelo in the Matachines dance, and his son Rudy Junior played the abuela in the Matachín dance before his death at age thirty-five.)

Esequiel's niece has yet to come back to perform the Matachines dance, but the collection of coronas and other accouterments of the ritual are still lovingly cared for, waiting for the day when the troupe will reassemble.

I finally got hold of Alonzo, Esequiel's son, to ask about his magnificent white horse, whose name Esequiel didn't know. Alonzo assures me that the horse, now fourteen years old, is doing fine. Alonzo breeds him regularly, and the horse is in great demand because of his high spirit and Arabian bloodline. His name is Apache. Mom and I stopped by the corrals to see him, and he is as spirited as ever.

Salomón's house on the hill caught on fire. His daughter Sylvia pulled him out before it burned to the ground. When I stopped to visit him recently, he asked for a new copy of the photo I'd given him of him and his Chihuahua, who perished in the flames.

Patricio Martínez, my compadre on the water board, has grown suddenly forgetful, a victim of Alzheimer's, they say. He didn't recognize me when I stopped to see him recently, although talk of his cows out in the pasture by Don Patricio Cruz's house brought an animated smile to his face—and much discussion about the cows' recent antics.

Juan Trujillo is still planting his fields. On my most recent visit, he informed me that he had just put in his alverjones (peas). As we talked, he called to his wife, Antonia, to bring a tortilla and some *miel de caña* (sorghum molasses) for my mother, who was sitting in the car waiting for me. While she munched down the warm homemade tortilla and sighed at the familiar flavor of the miel (which Juan had squeezed using an old horse-drawn press), Juan practiced the art of the affectionate insult on me. "*Ya los jóvenes no valen ni dos reales.*—Nowadays young men aren't worth a quarter," he said. "*¡Como tú! Tú no eres ni la mitad de hombre como era su abuelo Abedón.*—Like you! You aren't half the man your grandpa Abedón was," he fairly sneered at me. "*O tampoco don Reyes, quien era ranchero y tejedor también.*—Or your great-grandpa Don Reyes, who was a farmer and a weaver, too." But then, after this scolding, Juan proceeded to quietly tell me his dream of someday bringing young children to his farm and teaching them how to plant and maintain a garden.

Benerito is glad to be retired from the county and spending time at home, with his two sisters and brother nearby. On a recent visit, his sisters Agapita and Martha cooked for Benerito and me a spectacular meal of chile, beans, *chicos*, and green beans, all from their garden. They heaped the food onto savory buñuelos that they made while I visited with Benereito—reminding me repeatedly that these were buñuelos and NOT sopaipillas, that "new" dish that is so popular in restaurants.

My mother celebrated her ninety-first birthday, and we're still making trips to Chimayó to call on the viejitos, but she can't get her chicharrón burritos at Leona's anymore, since Leona closed her restaurant. We make our annual pilgrimage for chile and stop at the Rancho often. And we make our visits to the santuario and the campo santo to pay respects and remember our antepasados.

Time moves to a different rhythm in Chimayó. Since I began this project, several homicides and drug deaths have been reported in the papers, and there have been countless visits for miraculous healings and spiritual rebirths at the santuario. A new proposal to develop a retreat center at the santuario has spurred great debate and prompted citizens to organize in order to try to steer development in Chimayó. In cooperation with Santa Fe County, they've drafted a community plan for Chimayó, a blueprint for future development that would recognize and protect important historic sites, like the Santuario de Chimayó and the Plaza del Cerro.

Even as the Plaza del Cerro continues to run down, the history museum there, managed by the Chimayó Cultural Preservation Association, is prospering and sponsoring programs to celebrate the place's deep history and to promote traditional arts and crafts. The association is planning to put on a Matachines dance at the plaza for Día de San Buenaventura, the feast day for the plaza's patron saint. This will be the first time Matachines have danced there since Esequiel and his group did many years ago. It won't be a troupe from Chimayó, but instead a group from the East Mountain area near Albuquerque, but all are hopeful it will bring back the magic of the dances once performed by Chimayosos.

Nothing changes and yet everything changes in Chimayó, subtly and slowly. I've been watching and experiencing this for over fifty years. Chimayó is already far removed in lifestyle from the days when I ran around there as a child, and even farther from the time when dichos informed everyday life. Still, the flavor of those times lingers, and even now I love to walk in the hills and visit with people in town. I've come to know a larger community than ever before, a place full of good people with big hearts. In this, I've confirmed dear Grabielita's favorite saying, *"En este mundo no hay ningún corazón desocupado.*—In this world there isn't an empty heart." Like all dichos, this has layers of meaning, but fundamentally it acknowledges the goodness inherent in every person.

Most of the fine people my mother and I have met in this six-year ramble around Chimayó aren't mentioned in this account, not because they didn't tell good stories or offer fine characters to profile. They all did, and we've been astonished by the kindness extended to us, by the candid, openhearted welcomes we've received. To all of those whom I didn't mention, and to those whom I do, *¡gracias a todos!*

We've also seen that many Chimayosos are facing difficult times and are struggling with numerous troubles. But these families have been there a long time and have survived profound challenges—and they're still there. Their resiliency derives from an innate toughness and an unbending faith, but also reflects the love, wisdom, and humor that are deeply salted into the culture—and so clearly expressed in these durable dichos. They've kept people smiling and thinking and hanging on.